THE DIGITAL FILM EVENT

OTHER BOOKS BY TRINH T. MINH-HA

Cinema Interval, 1999

Drawn from African Dwellings
In collaboration with Jean-Paul Bourdier, 1996

Framer Framed, 1992

When the Moon Waxes Red: Representation, Gender and Cultural Politics, 1991

Woman Native Other: Writing Postcoloniality and Feminism, 1989

En minuscules. Book of poems, 1987

African Spaces: Design for Living in Upper Volta
In collaboration with Jean-Paul Bourdier, 1985

Un Art sans oeuvre, 1981

THE DIGITAL
FILM EVENT

Trinh T. Minh-ha

ROUTLEDGE
NEW YORK AND LONDON

Published in 2005 by
Routledge
Taylor & Francis Group
270 Madison Avenue
New York, NY 10016

Published in Great Britain by
Routledge
Taylor & Francis Group
2 Park Square
Milton Park, Abingdon
Oxon OX14 4RN

Printed in the United States of America on acid-free paper
10 9 8 7 6 5 4 3 2 1

International Standard Book Number-10: 0-415-97224-8 (Hardcover) 0-415-97225-6 (Softcover)
International Standard Book Number-13: 978-0-415-97224-6 (Hardcover) 978-0-97225-3 (Softcover)

Library of Congress Cataloging-in-Publication Data

Catalog record is available from the Library of Congress

Taylor & Francis Group
is the Academic Division of T&F Informa plc.

Visit the Taylor & Francis Web site at
http://www.taylorandfrancis.com

and the Routledge Web site at
http://www.routledge-ny.com

CONTENTS

PART III
JAPAN: ALTERITY AND THE IMAGE EFFECT

PART IV
INSTALLATIONS

ILLUSTRATIONS, FILMOGRAPHY AND DISTRIBUTION

ILLUSTRATIONS AND FILMOGRAPHY

Photo design, layout and installation drawings by: Jean-Paul Bourdier.
Front cover artwork: *A Small Step for a Fish* by Jean-Paul Bourdier
All photos in parts I, II, and III are from *The Fourth Dimension*. Photos related to the installations are specified accordingly. Photos of body art and land art in the desert are by Jean-Paul Bourdier ("Which side?" "Stone Alphabet" and "Heat")

Night Passage. 2004. 98 mins. Digital. Color. Women Make Movies; DnC Media.

The Fourth Dimension. 2001. 87 mins. Digital. Color. Women Make Movies; Freunde der Deutschen Kinemathek; British Film Institute; DnC Media.

A Tale of Love. 1995. 108 mins. Color. Distributed by: Women Make Movies; Freunde der Deutschen Kinemathek; British Film Institute; Image Forum; DnC Media. (Print with Chinese subtitles at the Golden Horse Taipei Film Festival Archives.)

Shoot for the Contents. 1991. 102 mins. Color. Distributed by: Women Make Movies; Image Forum; National Film & Video Lending Service; DnC Media.

Surname Viet Given Name Nam. 1989. 108 mins. Color and B & W. Distributed by: Women Make Movies; British Film Institute; Freunde der Deutschen Kinemathek; Third World Newsreel; MOMA (New York); Image Forum; National Film & Video Lending Service; Korean Film Archive; DnC Media.

Naked Spaces - Living Is Round. 1985, 135 mins. Color. Distributed by: Women Make Movies; British Film Institute; Freunde der Deutschen Kinemathek; MOMA (New York); Lightcone; National Film & Video Lending Service; DnC Media.

Reassemblage, 1982. 40 mins. Color. Distributed by: Women Make Movies; Third World Newsreel; British Film Institute; Freunde der Deutschen Kinemathek; MOMA (New York); Lightcone; Image Forum; National Film & Video Lending Service; DnC Media.

DISTRIBUTION

British Film Institute
21 Stephen Street
London W1T 1LN
Tel: +44 (0) 20 7255 1444
Fax: +44 (0) 20 7436 7950
www.bfi.org.uk

DnC Media
2F Shinwoo BLDG,
226-3 Nonhyun-Dong, Kangnam-Gu,
Seoul 135-010 Korea
Tel: +82-2-518-4332
Fax: +82-2-518-4333
Email: John Go
   <kinoman@dncmedia.com>

Freunde der Deutschen Kinemathek
im Filmhaus
Potsdamer Str. 2
10785 Berlin, Germany
Tel: (030) 269 55 142
Fax: (030) 269 55 111
Email: mg@fdk-berlin.de

Image Forum
2-10-2 Shibuya, Shibuya-ku
Tokyo, 150-0002, Japan
Tel: 81(0)3 5766-1119
Fax: 81(0)3 5466-0054
Email: yms@imageforum.co.jp
www.imageforum.co.jp

Korean Film Archive
Acquisition & Preservation Division
Acquisition Dept.
700, Seocho-Dong, Seocho-Gu,
Seoul, 137-718 Korea
Tel: 82-2-521-3147 (ext. 133)
Fax: 82-2-582-6213
Email: Hyeyun jeong
   <hyjeong@koreafilm.or.kr>

Lightcone
12 rue des Vignoles
75020 Paris, France
Tel: 33 (1) 4659 0153
Fax: 33 (1) 4659 0312
Email: sophie.laurent@lightcone.org

National Film & Video Lending Service
Cinemedia Access Collection
222 Park Street
South Melbourne 3205, Australia
Tel: (61 3) 99297044
Fax: (61 3) 99297027
Email: access@cinemedia.net

Museum of Modern Art
Circulating Film Library
11 W. 53rd St
New York, NY 10019
Tel: (212) 708-9530

Third World Newsreel
545 Eighth Avenue, 10th Floor
New York, NY 10018
Tel: (212) 947-9277
Fax: (212) 594-6417
Email: twn@twn.org
www.twn.org

Women Make Movies
462 Broadway, Suite 503K
New York, NY 10013
Tel: (212) 925-0606
Fax: (212) 925-2052
Email: orders@wmm.com
www.wmm.com

ACKNOWLEDGMENTS

It was initially thanks to the generosity of my hosts in Japan that the research work for *The Fourth Dimension* was made possible. My gratitude goes to Professor Kobayashi Fukuko from Waseda University; Professors Hara Hiroko, Tachi Kaoru and Takemura Kazuko from the Institute for Gender Studies at Ochanomizu University, where I taught as Visiting Professor; and Professor Ryuta Imafuku from Tokyo University of Foreign Studies. I also wish to thank all the interviewers involved, as well as the editors and publishers who have given permission to reprint the interviews. Special thanks are further due to Carolyn Pan and to Michelle Dizon for their assistance in the Photoshop work involved in the scanning and layout of the photographs. Last but not least, this book owes its existence, its look, and its rhythms to Jean-Paul Bourdier's dedicated art and design work.

PART I

TECHNOLOGY'S RITUALS

STILL SPEED

with Elizabeth Dungan

Dungan: *We work with being, but nonbeing is what we use," said Lao Tzu. Considering your move to the digital format, how might* The Fourth Dimension *relate to nonbeing, or emptiness?*

Trinh: It's great to open with Lao Tzu. Although that statement can be addressed in many ways in relation to my work, the fact that you relate it to the digital format and to *The Fourth Dimension* gives us a more specific direction.

The classic example for this I and not-I relation is that of a splendid cart whose wheels are made with a hundred spokes, and whose truth raises questions among Tao and Zen practitioners as follows: if one takes off both front and rear parts and remove the axle, then what will this grand cart be? The same question underlies the making of *The Fourth Dimension*, whose subject is not exactly Japan or Japanese culture, but the Image of Japan as mediated by the experience of "dilating and sculpting time" with a digital machine vision. What characterized the digital image is its inherent mutability—the constant movement of appearing and vanishing that underlies its formation. In today's electronic space of computerized realities, the sage's words would fare quite well, for one can hear in them all at once: the practical voice of ancient wisdom, the dissenting voice of postcoloniality, and the visionary voice of technology.

Paradoxically, being is not being, and nonbeing is not a negation of being. The spokes' use for the cart is there where they are not. My work can be said to lie as much at the junction of form and content, as of form and no form. What are intensely present on screen are there actually to address specific absences. Bringing into visibility the invisible would only gain in scope and in dimension if, for example, the film takes as part of its subject of inquiry the invisible forces and relations at work in the creative process. The challenge is to find a way to let the film perform the holes, the gaps, and the specific absences by which it takes shape. Sound and silence, movement and stillness are also not opposed to one another. Silence can speak volumes, especially when it is both individual and collective. Sometimes in speech one clearly hears silence and sometimes what one says is a form of silence. Just as awareness in non-action is the texture that defines a sage's every action, the musical quality of an instrument and its ability to resonate largely depend upon its internal emptiness.

In the visualizing of Japan, the non-Japan is constantly activated. As it is said, presence gives each event its values, but absence makes it work. For me, realizing a film in the highly advanced technological and economical context of Japan is, in a way, to move ahead into the age of digital compositing so as to return anew to the initiatory power of "pathmaking." (A term, as stated in the film, used in reference to the name of a Korean refugee who initially introduced the art of gardens in Japan as we know it today. The outside- or the non-Japan is here defining the inside-Japan—what we identify as characteristically Japanese). Such power can be found, for example, in the many existential arts of Japanese culture: the craft of framing time, the skill of behavior, the rites of daily activities, the way of land and water, the calligraphy of visual and architectural environment, or else the time performances of social and theatrical life.

Images of the real, produced at the speed of light, are made to play with their own reality as images. There, where new technology and ancient Asian wisdom can meet in all "artificiality" is where what is viewed as the objective reality underneath the uncertain world of appearance proves to be no more no less than a reality effect—or better, a being time. With digital systems taking part in our everyday thought and work, and with the advent of virtual reality, we are witnessing a profound reality shift, one that radically impacts upon the foundations of our knowledge, and upon our perception of the world.

D: *Your response, and your attentiveness to presence and absence, seems to resonate with the very process of digitalization: a translation into a series of zeros and ones, or "on and off." The underlying foundation of 01010101 relates to these productive couplings of being and nonbeing, absence and presence. In fact, with the digital medium, one can never isolate a "still" image: the image seen on screen is always "in the making" or always incomplete—partially present and partially absent. You've written elsewhere about the cinema's limits. How might* The Fourth Dimension *transcend, resist, or revise these limits? Can you describe, for example, the role of color in your digital work?*

T: I've spoken at length on the limits of established categories in cinema. These categories—narrative, documentary, experimental—define the way a film is made and received, and hence its limits. Rather than coming back to these, I will expand a bit on the limits of the visual, the verbal and the musical that constitute cinema's fabric. Although these three realms are tightly related in my films and are created with similar principles and concerns, they also remain independent in their processes. In deciding "what cinema is all about," any tendency to favor one of these realms over the other and to establish a relation of domination in which ear, mouth or hand is subordinated to eye, for example, would precipitate one's encounter with the medium's limits—if one works intimately with it. The question then is not so much to transcend as to discern them, so as to work with each of them independently and interactively. And the challenge is to operate right at the edge of what is and what no longer is "cinema."

Cinema is commonly thought of as being essentially visual. As it is practiced in the film industry and in the experimental arena, digital cinema tends to reinforce such a definition, even though the two milieux may differ radically in their eye-dominant treatment of film. On the one hand, you have the story-image—an image *re-produced* so as to advance the plot or to illustrate the story most efficaciously—and on the other, you have the painting-image—an image activated in its plastic form, or *de-formed* and made unrecognizable so as to claim its status as pure vision. Steeped in photographic

realism and representation, the former has been referred to as being "anti-visual" by those who abide by the latter but, as I've discussed elsewhere, I find more relevant the difference made between working in the visual mode, for which legibility is central, and in the image mode, for which alterity is the defining factor. In other words, one may look at images with eyes wide open and yet not see the image and its nature.

Today, altering, dis-figuring, animating, morphing and trans-shaping the familiar in the image has become most popular, thanks to computer technology. Digital production and postproduction have opened doors at many levels in filmmaking, but the one I will briefly mention here is that of special effects. There's much talk about digital media restoring to us what has been repressed in cinema: visual techniques relegated to the realm of animation and of special effects. Shooting live-action footage is now just a small step in the process. The recorded image has been used primarily as raw material for further compositing. Reality has become "elastic." The digital format, which is much more capacious and compressible, hence more flexible and versatile than analog, is not only offering a bridge between film and video; it is also displacing fixed boundaries set up between film and animation or computer games, for example. If today's Hollywood blockbusters are driven by special effects, digital experimental wizardry is obsessed with effects that appeal first and foremost to the retina.

The Fourth Dimension departs from such popularized expectation because its approach to new technology neither indulges in the virtuosity of special retinal effects nor does it rely on distorting, fracturing, or transfiguring images in order to defamiliarize the subject it is engaged with. On the contrary, what partly constitutes the unseen dimension underlying the images offered of Japan is the mutability of relations between the ordinary, the extraordinary and the infraordinary as captured in the mutability of the digital image itself. To call attention to the creative process in the instance of consumption, I did something very simple: I added layers—layers often made visible as they come at precise moments, in selected shapes and colors on top of the image. Working intensely with what I used to hate in video—the unavoidable moiré and iris effects that are exacerbated by video light, and a tabooed color such as bright red, in relation to green—I also emphasize the lightness and portability of the camera in the shooting phase. (The movement of a camera carried on the shoulder is very different from that of a camera held in the palm of one's hand.) Images are thus shown in their shifting light and traveling motion as well as in their temporal sequencing and mobile framing.

Viewers have commented on the way the screen is turned into a canvas in *The Fourth Dimension*. As one said, "I like the hand-held shifts. You are painting and veiling with lights as you move." Although I think that digital compositing has presented us with a host of capabilities in working with the painterly image, I am not at all working under the specter of painting, as a number of experimental filmmakers tend to do. Rather than using digital technology to reinforce the domination of the visual and the retina in cinema, one can certainly use it to propel image making into other realms of the senses and of awareness. Compositing in multiple layers is one of the features in digital editing, whose inventive potential is most appealing, not merely in the crafting of images, but even more so in the designing of sound. This is the one process I truly enjoy while working on the film. The possibilities are indefinite. While I was trained as a music composer, I prefer to work with the local people's music for the sound track, to which I add improvised music realized by Greg Goodman, who played the prepared piano and a range of other musical objects; and by Shoko Hikage, who performed both the Japanese vocals and the bass Koto. To work with their music not as finished pieces, but as "unedited" sounds the way I work with unedited footage in the montage process—dismantling, splitting, inserting, layering, spacing, joining, trimming and repeating—is a way of continuing their improvisation work in old and new rhythms. This is exciting and very demanding because improvisation requires that we become first and foremost "listeners" in our creations (as differentiated from "sound makers" for example). New technology has made working with audio tracks so much easier. It has given me a lot of freedom in designing sound.

Further, my films are conceived musically—as light, rhythm and voice. I've spoken at length elsewhere on the determining role that rhythm plays in social, ethical and political relations. In *The Fourth Dimension*, I can say, for example, that the two main "characters" and the two most powerful rhythms that I've experienced during my stay in Japan are: the train, as it regulates time (the time of traveling and of viewing); and the drum, as it is the beat of (our) life (significantly played by women in the film). The role of music, especially the one performed for the film, is not merely to underscore the action or the visual, but to create a multifunctional space in which many relations between seen and heard are possible. Rather than producing linear, homogenized time, digital sound designing allows me to work intensely with *other* speeds, those that come not only with the diverse motions in an image, but also with stillness, or with an image emptied of visible action.

D: *You've described before the ways that artists in ancient China might focus equally on mountains, persimmons, or horses, highlighting the ways in which none of these are static. Nature is always in the course of things. In contrast, representation, by its own "nature," is an arrested moment, but the quality it represents is always in flux. Can you expand on these insights?*

T: Very nice link. For me, filmmaking is really working with relations in the play of senses—among the ear, eye, and hand; the present and the absent, the different elements of cinema; among filmmaker, filmed subject and film viewer; as well as among components of the cinematic apparatus. Relationships are not simply given. They are constantly in formation—undone and redone as in a net whose links are indefinite. And working on relationships is working with rhythm—the rhythms, for example, that determine people's daily interactions; the dynamics between sound and silence; or the way an image, a voice, a music relates to one another and acts upon the viewer's reception of the film. Rhythm is a way of marking and framing relationships. Through music, we learn to listen to our own biorhythms; to the language of a people, the richness of silence; and hence to the vast rhythm of life.

This is how I see the link with the tradition of Asian arts, which you evoke in your question. In working with other speeds, the singular and the plural meet on the canvas of time. Artists of ancient China decided, for example, to devote themselves singlemindedly to only bamboo, bird, tree, persimmon or orchid painting during their entire lifetimes. This is not a question of "expertise" as we know it today. If they paint mountains all their lives, it's not because they want to become an expert in mountains.

Rather, I would say, it's because they receive the world through mountains. Even if one comes to exactly the same place and looks from the same point of view everyday, the mountain is never the same. It would change every single second. In other words, there is no such thing as "dead nature" or what in the tradition of Western arts is considered a still life.

There is no concept of *nature morte* in ancient Eastern Art. Nature is alive, always shifting. It should be shown in its course. So you can draw thousands of mountains and you can devote your life to painting this single subject, yet each painting shows a unique mountain-instance. Painting here is inscribing the ever-changing processes of nature—that are also one's own. Painter and painted are, in a way, both caught on canvas in the act of painting. To paint nature is to paint one's self-portrait. (Although the tradition of Western arts tends to be anthropocentric, Francis Bacon's self-portraits can be said to be similar in spirit). So this is one way of taking in the world: being so intimately in touch with oneself that every time one returns deep inside, one opens wide to the outside world.

The other approach, which my work may seem at first to exemplify, is to work with multiplicity in an outward traveling mode. But such a distinction is temporary, because ultimately, the two approaches do meet and merge as in my case. I travel from one culture to another—Senegalese, West African, Vietnamese, Chinese and Japanese—in making my films. This may fit well with today's transnational economy, in which the crossing of geophysical boundaries is of wide occurrence, whether by choice or by political circumstances. But for the notion of the transversal and the transcultural to take on a life in one's work, traveling would have to happen also in one place, or inward. One can evoke here the depth of time, a notion that is particularly relevant to digital reality. Home and abroad are not opposites when traveling is not set against dwelling and staying home. In a creative context, coming and going can happen in the same move, and traveling is where I am. Where you are is where your identity is; that's your place, your home and your being now.

D: *Constructions of time, and re-imaginings of time, seem to be an important aspect of your work. How might traveling conjure this notion of time and relate it to space? I am also thinking here of one of Paul Virilio's books entitled* The Lost Dimension. *Among other things, this book explores an accelerated perspective, a discussion of vanishing points, a sense of displacement, the doubling of space and time. For these and other reasons, Virilio's work seems very resonant with your own. Given this rhyming of titles between* The Fourth Dimension *and* The Lost Dimension, *how might you describe your work in relationship to Virilio's work?*

T: Although I've not thought of Virilio in choosing the title—which refers primarily to the dimension of time, of light and of "non-being"—your association is very relevant and refreshing, especially in view of the more common tendency to associate my films with Chris Marker's films, and this one in particular with *Sans Soleil*.

I've expanded earlier on how, in weaving this mutable light tapestry that is film, I work with uneven and heterogeneous speeds, rather than with a homogenized space of linear time. This can be related to Virilio's discussion of the lost dimension. Without trying to summarize what he wrote with eloquence, I'll just mention here a few relevant threads. In the constitution of digital images, Virilio notes that the electronic eye

indifferently scans a landscape and an image of that landscape. There's a fusion of the actual and the simulated that springs from the deterioration of physical dimensions and analogical representations of space. Thus, the depth of space he defines as that of the field of surfaces available to direct observation is being replaced by the depth of time that he sees in the indirect recording of numerical data. Speed becomes the vector for electronic representation, and the crisis of the physical dimension in the age of electronic telecommunications is apparently a crisis of substantive, continuous, homogeneous space. What one has instead is a discontinuous, heterogeneous space in which the accidental becomes essential. Today the primal dimension is the dimension of speed time, which defies both temporal and physical measurements.

In the move from matter to light, scientific knowledge, benefiting from the most advanced technologies, relies less and less on material evidences or solid reference points. Virilio's critique of this "cinematism of scientific representation" is linked to his critique of a form of decentralization that comes with the advent of a postindustrial "endo-colonialism" (as distinguished from the exo-colonialism of central Empires in the industrial age), in which separatist political regimes promote the creation of colonies in their own territories or their own sites—colonies deprived of agricultural and industrial resources, and sometimes, more importantly, of their own water sources. The center of cyberworld is everywhere and nowhere, and the tragedy of this virtual de/centralization is that it delocalizes work and our relation to the other. Virilio has been working obsessively at this junction of science, technology, aesthetics and politics. With the rich body of work he has produced, his critical analyses should be understood, not as a condemnation of new technology, but as a criticism of the very object of his love.

In my "speeding through Japan's likeness" (a statement from *The Fourth Dimension*) and critical journey into Japan's times, I have many affinities for Virilio's critical stance. Despite my questioning take on Japan's coded insularity as related to the issue of *programmed agency* in screen space and televisual time, I love the site of my inquiry; the culture, the people and their practices. In cinema, a number of filmmakers working intensely with the power of the image in conveying the worthless, the banal and the negligible have insisted that one should get rid of the illusion of the third dimension (illusory depth of field—as in Hollywood's film realism) and produce flat, two-dimensional images that open to the fourth and fifth dimensions of Time and Spirit. Films that work with both the temporalities in the image and with the image as time-form allow us to experience not motion, but time as a form of its own. It is with a similar approach that *The Fourth Dimension* is realized, although as mentioned, I work with both the ordinary and the extraordinary. It is not a question of restoring the importance of the banal over the special and the exceptional, but to work with the inherent relations between the two. Rather than promoting a greater depth of field, as in the case of film, digital technology offers the possibility of working intensely with time and with the indefinite coexisting layers of past, present, and future.

Tradition and modernity, what I call Noh time and train time in the film, meet in a problematic but striking light on this virtual "canvas." Time is liquid in *The Fourth Dimension*. Sometimes it is experienced in its gaseous, melting, running forms, other times it is apprehended in its frozen, hardened, and divisive forms, and other times yet, it is presented as a stop-interval, with the familiar set of chronological naming and dating. The pull between a so-called loss of reality and an excess of reality leads to what Virilio terms the third interval, the interval of speed-light that is neither temporal nor spatial. I call such interval "Women's Time," as possibly defining Japan's Time: an interval in the film, "where in the heart of an insular culture, even the mobile world of invisible narrators, of uneven times and odd rhythms finds its place in the precise framing of daily activities" (quoted from *The Fourth Dimension*).

We are here at the edge of nature and culture, somewhere between the human, the animal, the vegetal, the machine, and the spiritual. Somewhere between the desire for augmented reality and remote control, and the need for a simple undivided way with the world. On the one hand, there is the move toward virtual perfection—the virtuality of high definition. On the other hand, there is a plural return among leading Western thinkers to the light of ancient Asian wisdom. For, rather than letting the old opposition between mind and body take a new lease on life with the perfection of virtual power, Asian thought often refers to the Snare of Illusion in which mortals are caught by their own doings. As a quote of Zen master Dogen says at the end of *The Fourth Dimension*, "the entire world is our mind," to which he also added, "the mind of a flower."

D: *In thinking about your work as exhibited in the context of Documenta 11 (2002), how would you describe the relationship between politics and aesthetics in your films?*

T: This relationship is always present in my work. But to continue our discussion on images and reality effect, politics is there where "we work with being." We are all engaged in the rituals in our everyday—the rituals of social life or of technology—but by remaining unaware of their artistic propensity, we remain caught in conformity. Rituals treated as rituals the way I did in *The Fourth Dimension* allow one to turn an instrument into a creative tool and to step out of the one-dimensional, technologically servile mind. For such a path of change, there is no short cut. In this age of infomania, where one can travel endlessly in cyberspace, efficacy and rapidity of means of reproduction and destruction require that reaction times be shortened and reflection times almost nonexistent. But when events happen so fast that one becomes a witness before realizing it, one is bound to slow down and to take one's time.

Information retrieval systems dominate and convenience often beats quality. There is a growing obsession with data without much concern for perspective and significance. With a mind set upon information, we develop the habit of *collecting* knowledge bits, often believing that literacy, culture, and politics are a matter of having the facts and evidences right at our fingertips. We demand that everything be at our disposal and expect access to be immediate and simultaneous—hence, our fascination with programs that promote instantaneous multidriving and multitasking. Such a power gained at the price of our direct involvement with people, events, and things is part of the profound syndrome of our information age. As convenience can, more often than not, be punishing to both form and content, concerns for integrity and substance are likely to be replaced by the need for hi-tech-looking programs that allow one to make "power points with bullets to followers." The pervasive attitude of commercialism has been turning every event into a sales pitch.

Slowness as a strategy of resistance is much needed in the speed of urban routine life. The film *Naked Spaces – Living is Round*, which was selected for exhibition at

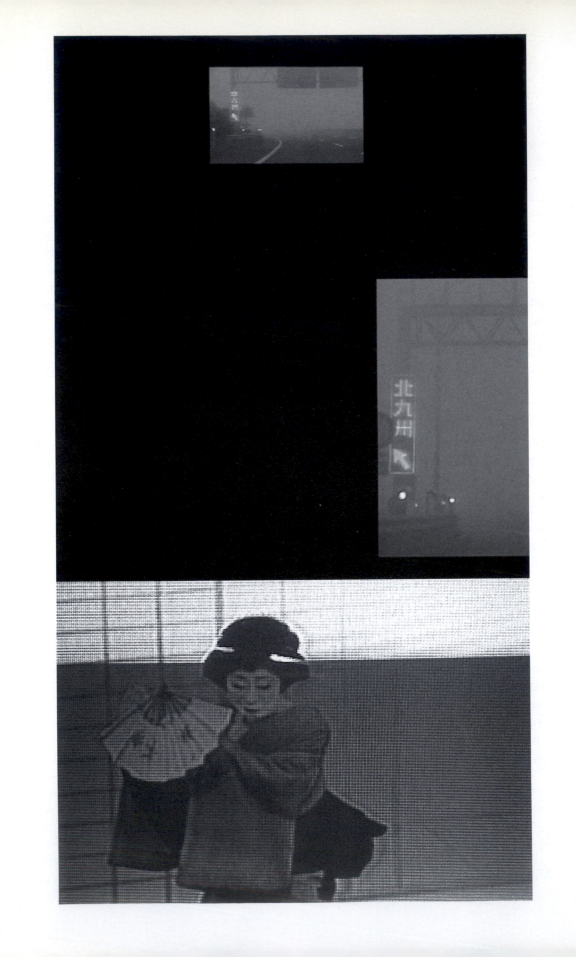

Documenta 11 together with three other films of mine (*Reassemblage, Surname Viet Given Name Nam,* and *Shoot for the Contents*) can certainly be seen as an ode to slowness. Or to the daily rhythms of the peoples of West Africa. Not only do the lengths of my films raise issues in the world of experimental films, but the way I work with film as time (rather than film as movement), and the way duration, temporalities, rhythms, and other elements of cinema are treated as inseparable from the subject shown also make the experience of film quite excruciating for impatient viewers. The time here is neither that of information or of entertainment. As a statement in *The Fourth Dimension* reminds, "Keep to the time as required by television; screen space, say TV programmers, is always, always limited. But, as novelist Hisashi Inoue once said, 'I don't like bonsaiism . . . it's perfectly alright for some trees to grow big and wild.'"

In times of coercive politics and transnational terror, slowing down so as to learn to listen anew is a necessity. For me this is particularly relevant, as I turn to digital systems in my last two films, *The Fourth Dimension* and *Night Passage.* For the question is not so much to produce a *new image* as to provoke, to facilitate, and to solicit a *new seeing.* Science without conscience, politics without ethics, technology without poetry result in deadly short-circuits. We've had to learn this, not only through disastrous political events, but more intimately through one's own body when it is under stress—the wired-up body that takes months to wind down, to recover, or to find its own rhythm. Non-being is what we use in working with being . . . when we start taking care of this utter silence, life speaks to us in a different language, one in which we catch glimpses of stillness in movement and feel movement arising in stillness. Velocity in stillness. Some viewers have spoken at length on such dynamics and on what they see as unexpected moments of stillness in the midst of rapid cuts and movements in *The Fourth Dimension.* Speed is here not opposed to slowness, for it is in stillness that one may be said to truly find speed. And rather than merely going against speed, stillness contains speed and determines its quality. Speed at its best in digital imaging is *still speed.* The speed of a flower mind.

D: *Dogen's sense of the "mind of a flower" seems to relate to your works' ode to slowness: there is an unveiling, an unfurling of layers across an extended and sometimes imperceptible time. How might this "vegetal" mindset relate to your interest in a "new seeing?" How might your re-conceptualization of production and reception, of creating and viewing, be a political intervention? Perhaps you can discuss Okwui Enwezor's approach to display and exhibition in Documenta, and the context in which your work was produced and received.*

T: It takes me some time to fully answer your question because there's the politics of production and reception, and there's the politics of exhibition. Documenta, Kassel's museum of 100 days, is a colossal cultural manifestation—significantly held in a small, remote town of the German countryside. Documenta can be said to be initially conceived as a break with a whole tradition of art exhibition, as well as a challenge to the art establishment of the Nazi totalitarian regime. However, as a large-scale transnational exhibition, Documenta's ambivalent participation in the marketing of global culture today is always under critical scrutiny. Although both Documenta 10 and 11 are conceived as counterglobalization efforts. The former was blamed, for example, for having widely ignored Eastern Europe and other parts of the world, and hence for failing to question the domineering role Western art assumes for itself, despite the director's proclaimed emphasis on the political context of aesthetic production. Documenta 11, curated by Enwezor, seems to be the first to act on that imperial framework, to insist on the processes of cultural mixing around the world (including Latin America, Africa, and Palestine), and to address questions of transcultural and transdiasporic practices.

Many of the artists selected there are those whose art I respect and really wish to see. I was particularly elated by the inclusion of African and Palestinian artists. In other words, my work was in good company; although not surprisingly, despite its being placed in an art-circuit, which is quite different from the film-festival circuit I am used to, it remains largely at odds with the art world, invisible to its historians and critics. Film's inclusion as one of the "arts" (or "fields of cultural production," as they are now called) to be presented at Documenta is only a recent phenomenon. On the other hand, the film industry, the Hollywood-ish film world as well as the PBS world of information, likes to speak contemptuously of everything it categorizes as "art film." To the marketing mind that dominates media production, any film that is noncommercial by nature is not really a film. An "art film" immediately means failure at the box office. So usually, the film world does not really want to be associated with the art world. And filmmakers whose works shuttle across these boundaries are very few. There is a tradition of experimental filmmaking that situates itself in the art context, but that body of work does not cross the line.

I have no stake in the "art film"—a category that, like any other film category (the documentary, the feature narrative, the avant-garde), is sometimes used to include my films, other times to exclude them, and often to their disadvantage. This, mainly because, while my films deal with the creative tools and the properties of cinema, they do so with a social and political view of both form and content. Furthermore, the form arrived at—which is also the content, and vice-versa—cannot be consumed merely as form, since what it addresses is its own fragile becoming, its nothingness, and hence, infiniteness. In defying categories, the body of work I produce meets with numerous rejections while it also gets to show widely in very diverse and controversial contexts. But even when it is given exposure, it tends to be marginalized within the very category it is given—or worse, within its own areas of strength.

Such a situation cannot be blamed solely on programmers or on the world of compartmentalization in which we live. Radically, it also has to do with the nature of my films. For example, as discussed earlier, there are at least three textual layers or three voices in my work: the visual text, the musical text, and the verbal text. But within the verbal layer itself, there are already at least two texts: one relating to the subject that is being visualized (like West Africa, Viet Nam, China, or Japan), and one speaking to the unfolding process of producing images and meanings. In other words, the commentary has a direct or indirect relation with the culture visualized, but it always also tells us something about the "how" of creativity—rather than the "what," since meaning is in flux. And by doing so, it questions its own politics of representation and positions the filmmaker. I'm constantly exposing where I stand.

With such a critical exposure, I am bound to lose power (it's just a trick; an illusion; an image; a film, after all . . . a nothing); because exposure of the work in its very

act of coming to being is exposure of the limit of a medium and a form of mediation. Media people usually do everything to make the story or the message they present appear seamless so as to bypass their own subjectivity. They are afraid the exposure will impoverish what they have to say, but actually it can really enrich it. Vulnerability can enhance our receptivity, and as we situate and position ourselves in what we do, there is no need for conflict. Rather than having to wage war in a relation of dominance and submission (of who's to remain on top) or of complementarity (the way one gender is expected to complement the other, for example), we can thrive and grow in a relation of multiplicity. To be an other among others can be a profoundly transformative experience.

Questions of racism, sexism, homo- and xeno-phobia, or whatever more phobia we have in our society, all have to do with the way we conceive of relationship. And there's a difference between seeing oneself as a link in the net and being subjected to comparisons of oneself to others. Let's take, for example, the notion of the intercultural, which has been promoted in the context of Documenta 11. The most common approach tends to be accumulative in its practice: one culture, one specialized knowledge is juxtaposed with another; members from different cultural fields come together to converse happily within their expertise. What gets glossed over in such an approach is the *inter-* itself. In adding, one has to learn to subtract, to let the holes speak and to work on the gap. The question is not that of putting two cultures together, or one next to the other. What is at stake in this inter-creation is the question of boundary and the very notion of the specialist and the expert. To cut across borders is to live aloud the malaise of categories and expertise. These would have to be thoroughly questioned and pushed to their limits so as to resist the comfort of belonging and of fixed classification.

The boundary zone then takes on its full function as the zone of transformation. Where, for example, does the boundary of Senegalese literature lie in the context of West, East and South Africa, and in relation to the literatures of specific Asian, European, or American cultures? When work is carried out across and in between domains, on that very boundary zone, the latter inevitably undergoes change. The encounter should lead to a transformation. This is a challenge most of us prefer not to take up because it is so much easier to continue to be an expert in our own field and consult another expert. It's difficult to let go of the barriers and let the challenge transform us. But for those of us who fare in a multiplicity of cultural fields, working in a transcultural inter-site that potentially belongs to everyone can be very enriching. It's a way of making links, of connecting, of expanding the net, rather than simply of asserting or reifying boundaries.

D: *In Documenta 11, your film* Naked Spaces: Living is Round *is situated amidst the work of Doris Salcedo's sculpture about absenting people in Columbia, Leon Golub's* Disappear You *and* We can Disappear You, *and Cildo Meireles'* Disappearing/Disappeared Element, *among others. How does absence figure in your own work?*

T: It's an interesting link you're making here. I've been addressing this question of absence in more inclusive terms in relation to Lao Tzu's non-being. We also touch on the digital image, which by its inherent mutability, plays with the disappearance of the real and invites the creative mind to conceive of the film event as a ritual performance of apparitions and disappearances. In this realm of the immaterial the accent is not so much on the spectacular appearances as on the underlying disappearances that happen with every appearance. Virilio's notion of cinematic time surfaces is here very relevant, and so is the distinction he made between the aesthetics of the appearance of a stable image and the aesthetics of dis-appearance of an unstable image. Rather than working with an event, in which form in their material support (the celluloid) emerges progressively, one faces here an event of accelerated disappearance.

One can shift to the social plane and infer from this discussion that the instability of a governmental regime is in proportion to the volume of political disappearances on which it thrives in order to rule. One way to link more specifically *Naked Spaces* to the works you mentioned is perhaps to discuss the question of cultural disappearance, which is different but not unrelated to the political disappearances in question. I am reminded here of what Toni Morrison said on how Africanism is intrinsic to Americanness; how black people remain the major referent in the framing of the Constitution even though they were never part of the deliberations that went into its making; or else, how certain white neighborhoods are defined by the spectacular absence of black people. I have been asked many times by members of the media establishment why I do not make a film on American culture, because they are very interested and this will most likely open doors for me in places where they have remained shut so far. But what I have been doing is not only reversing the situation as described by Morrison, I'm also taking the work further into the realm of the transcultural.

The absent, the underrepresented, the Third and Fourth World or the so-called disappearing cultures are the very appearances on which I prefer to spend my energy in making films and videos. But by doing so, I'm calling attention to the absent omni-presences of the dominant culture in our media practices, my own included. Again, Lao Tzu's words are very resonant here. In *Shoot for the Contents*, which I shot in China, I focus on the Dragon as an emblem of power and change. This majestic animal, whose names and appearances are numerous, has the capacity to "be as small as a silkworm or as large as the world." It has been time and again appropriated as a symbol of the ruler, and orders were issued during the Yuan dynasty, for example, to prohibit its apparitions in ordinary people's environments. But the people ignored such derisive orders because in fact, the dragon cannot be appropriated. In perpetual meta-morphoses, the animal continues to be this fabulous ever-changing creation of their imagination, diving deep, rising high, appearing and disappearing, in both male and female gender.

D: *Given the international collaboration of Documenta, along with the transfer of this work from 16 mm film to DVD, how might you describe the importance of translation to this show? How might you think about re-editing your work for multiple screens?*

T: People use the DVD format, which is a finishing format, mainly as a sales tool rather than as a distribution solution. In the case of Documenta, it's a slightly different story. Only *Naked Spaces* was transferred to DVD, because it showed in one of the main gallery spaces, actually in the Kulturbahnhof. The other films were screened in the film program that runs with the exhibition, in a regular movie theater. So the transfer has to do with the transfer of space, but also with a mode of viewing.

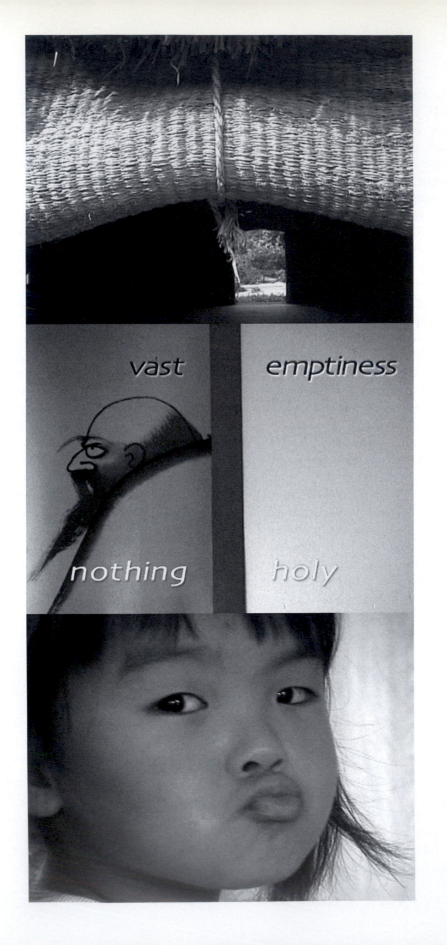

Naked Spaces is the longest film I've made so far (135 minutes), and its experience is largely determined by the quality of a certain absorption in duration. Viewers have compared it to an Indian *raga* (or "musical mode"). What seems most striking in the performances of music from India is the way they create an emotional climate and bring forth in the audience a specific emotional state. Here, the *alap* or "prelude" is just as important as the piece itself because the prelude is really the challenging moment when the musician improvises freely to go toward his or her audience and to literally tune in together. And that moment of both introduction and encounter between performer, listener and music can be as long as needed before it feels right for the piece to start. The raga can go on for hours and hours until dawn, and this is what my films have evoked—especially *Naked Spaces* because of its pace and length.

In the gallery space, the experience of duration may be lost, since viewers tend to come and go, and it's rare that people would sit there for over two hours. But because the film is shown continuously all day, it creates a different situation in which, for practical reasons, it is necessary to transfer it to DVD. Interestingly, this digital format allows one to return to a device linked with cinema's birth: the loop. The first showing of film was based on short loops. Today, the loop playback function on the DVD deck can be viewed as a mere technical device that automatically repeats the disk when it comes to the end of the film, or it can be viewed as a device that changes, structurally, the context and mode of viewing. Peter Kubelka, for example, who thought the ideal way to view his film *Unsere Afrikareise* is to have it looped and shown repeatedly again and again, would be happy here—although, ironically, he is said to be a purist and to hate the transfer of film to any other format.

The question of having more than one screen is also very relevant, because my films are all edited spatially and a film like *Naked Spaces*, with its length and expansive spaces, would benefit much from multiple projections and screens. Programmers who have exclaimed on the spatial quality of my films have also proposed that I work on that in future exhibitions. It will be a real treat for me, especially since I've thought all along, while editing my last film, *Night Passage*, about the potentials of a montage of the film for multiple screens in creating a different emotional field than the one conveyed by a single frontal screen. The issue of finance is looming large here, but I certainly have hopes.

TIMESURFING

with Kathrin Rhomberg

First published in the catalog "*Ausgetraeumt . . .*", by The
Secession, Vienna, Austria, 2001/2002

Rhomberg: *The exhibition "Ausgetraeumt . . .", deals with an assumed general
perception of today's political and social reality, as based on disillusionment. There
doesn't seem to be a readiness to even imagine a better world and society nowadays. How
do you personally think about the present and the future?*

Trinh: One can only answer this question by revisiting the terms of linear thinking
and linear time—the way we conceive of the past, the present, and the future. We
always think that to progress in certain ways is to go forward in a linear ordering of
things. But for me, this is where despair can settle in. For example, we hear from many
people who are attached to the radical struggles of the sixties how bad a time we are
living in right now—because the sixties were very alive and full of possibilities, whereas
today we are just caught in this moment of (no) history where there is no political
agenda, no creative thrust, only social amnesia and anorexia. I myself do not think of it
in that way.

Problems and issues change all the time, with each single moment. What we are
witnessing today . . . if we do not think in terms of linear progress, but rather in
terms of a spiraling, multidimensional here-and-now—where everything in the
present carries with it its past and its future. The seed of the future is always already
there, in the present, in the past. If we think of it in that way, inclusively rather than
exclusively, spatially and spirally rather than only linearly, then the time we live (in)
is rich and full of potential. It's just the way things are being directed that leads us to
the thought of impasse and to the helpless or cynical feeling that everywhere we
turn we meet with an impasse. We can see with current events that a lot of innovative solutions we've come up with at the peak of our technological performance can
actually be turned around and used against ourselves. Science without conscience is
self destructive.

Any tool of the oppressor can be turned against the oppressor. The high-powered tool devised to benefit oneself to the detriment of others ultimately also serves to destroy oneself and one's own kind. We do recurrently witness this kind of phenomena in our times. To use a common term in new media and technology—"surfing"— we have to know how to *surf* with the wave, without, however, falling into passive consumption. Receptivity does not necessarily means passivity. Being receptive can be most active. The full implications of new technologies elude us, for even though we devise the means, we don't really know how to deal with them when their use outruns our expectation.

It is very interesting that a Western man who went to Tibet to live and be ordained as a monk came to declare: "The man of the new millennium is not the man who conquers but the man who absorbs." I think the question of absorbing or receiving has to be seen really anew. In the art world, of course, this is something that artists are very tuned to. Most of them are like these acupuncture needles that feel, very acutely, the times. This comes from a certain availability—intense and caring—so that one is always absorbing and receiving creatively.

Everything devised as dictated by the marketing mind can be modified and displaced from its habitual orbit of commodity. Today, one cannot really talk about opposition or about a rupture with the past. One can understand the usefulness of an oppositional stance at certain moments of a struggle, but such a stance is more a strategy than an end, for it remains very much dependent on what it opposes. So here we are no longer talking about opposition, we are talking about subtle differences: all the modifications (in orientation, in social, ethical, and aesthetic dimension, for example), the fine line we have to make for ourselves between a goal that is mercantile, subjected to the marketing mind, and one that is creatively innovative, geared toward a different direction, profoundly transforming the way reality speaks to us.

R: *Some artists, especially those belonging to the generation of the sixties and seventies, are emphasizing that radical positions are not possible any more in our times. Do you agree with that?*

T: I tend to disagree. It all depends on how we define the term "radical." Some people are still very nostalgic for the sixties. This is understandable because it was a period of great transformation in history. But these people speak of radical-ness from a one-directional view, and in a way, they are not surfing with the time. What is radical for them relies on what appears rather "obvious" to us today. The rupture is so obvious, it bounces back within the same frame. Today when you do that, you immediately fall into a category. To oppose in order to fit comfortably into another category is to have no spirit of freedom. Clear-cut opposition thrives on what it opposes. "Radical" for me has to do with returning to something that is very basic. From the term itself, the movement is that of going back to the unseen root, of stripping down to the very basic and of changing from there. And in turning back to the vital and unformed, that is the root, we can't do away with the so-called past. We have to go there where memories of past and future lead us in order to effect change. Struggles of resistance and liberation, like the women's movement or the gay and lesbian movement for example,

human time
MACHINE TIME

are not struggles that can thrive on oppositions strategically set up; they are struggles that cross more than one border in modifying our consciousness. Hence the widespread introduction, for example, of the notion of the "trans-", something that goes over, that cuts both ways. "Transgender," "transpolitics," "transnational." All these "trans-" notions deal with the crossing. Rather than having to deny one side or the other, the crossing allows us more freedom of movement and hence, of no movement as well. We can shuttle back and forth, being more mobile in what we do, even though that mobility—as we can see in the current political world events—can be turned around against us as well.

Direct pointing
to the human heart
seeing one's nature becoming Buddha
Written by the 83-year-old
priest Hakuin
sitting beneath
the Sala tree without his glasses

THE CYBORG'S HAND: CARE OR CONTROL?

with *Valentina Vitali*

First published in *The Metro* (journal of film, television, radio, multimedia, Sydney, Australia) No 133, 2002. In her introduction, Vitali wrote: "Screened earlier this June at the Tate Modern, her [Trinh's] latest video, *The Fourth Dimension*, (2001, 87 min), was presented at the Locarno and Edinburgh Film Festivals, the Graz Biennale in Vienna, the New York Video Festival, the Asian American Film Festival and the Museum of Modern Art's Documentary Film Festival. The title alludes to time and the processes it involves: the traveler's subjective experience, the sacred time of ritual, mechanical time, film time. In this film-essay, Trinh T. Minh-ha immerses herself in contemporary Japan to examine the crystallised tensions between modernity and tradition, the present and the past, and the fusion of Eastern and Western cultures. Combining shots of cityscapes, ceremonies (funeral processions, theatre, religious festivals, and rituals) and everyday life, she delivers a reflection on the temporalities we live by. Avoiding any hint of didacticism, the documentary also explores the relation between sound and image, functioning as a recurrent melody that appeals to all senses."

Vitali: *I used to teach film theory to aspiring filmmakers. One day the students were told to find an idea for a documentary. One of the students—incidentally, a woman from Korea—said that she wanted to make a documentary about a dream she had dreamed, and proceeded to tell her dream. The teacher told her that she could not make a documentary about a dream because documentaries were about facts and reality. So, the following week the same student went to the teacher and, explaining that she had now found a good subject for her documentary, simply retold her story without, however, saying that it was her dream. This anecdote was told to me by my colleague, the teacher of the documentary module. His intention was to show me that some students really are confused. Contrary to my colleague, I thought that the student had grasped the central* *problematic of documentary filmmaking and, more generally, the problematic of realism. I wanted to start this interview with this anecdote because your work, and particularly* The Fourth Dimension, *questions the conventional boundary between fiction and documentary, by explicitly confronting the issue of narration, and therefore of history and temporality.*

Trinh: We keep encountering these classifications—fiction, documentary, and experimental—everywhere in the film world. I don't feel as if I belong to any of them. Even the terms art and avant-garde raise questions among artists. In making these distinctions, the tendency has often been to reiterate a preconceived hierarchy, and hence to harden a fundamentally explorative activity into a category of work. There is no real experiment when "experimental" becomes a genre of its own; "avant-" and "arrière-garde" are but the two sides of the same classification. In "documentary," one has to go through fiction to show reality, just as in fictional narratives, one has to go far into the realm of documentary to document one's own fiction. That's why, rather than endorsing these categories by which the film world largely abides, I produce films that I consider to be first and foremost "boundary events." One can view them as different ways of working with freedom in experiencing the self and the world.

The documentary aspect of *The Fourth Dimension* has less to do with the nonstaged nature of the material shot than with the process of documenting its own unfolding: it documents its own time, its creation in megahertz, the different paths and layers of time-light that are involved in the production of images and meanings. Our life situations are regulated by time—by instituted work time or television time, for example; our bodies and daily activities tell us with precision how time takes on specific forms and leaves its marks in our landscape. And yet, when I introduce the work as a video or a D-film[1] on time, it is like saying it is about nothing. This is a bit similar to the case of the student you just mentioned: a documentary has to be about something factual and verifiable. But, a sum of facts does not necessarily leads to truth.

Time defines and dominates new technology. It conditions every aspect of our lives and is often invoked as a criterion to determine the "quality" of media works. Films that are quickly dismissed as "too long" by film reviewers are often those that let us feel time in its operation and materialisation. So, when people tell me the subject of *The Fourth Dimension* is abstract . . . OK, but depending on how we live it, what is more concrete than time? Is "too long" an abstract reality? Film is time and if time is a fiction, so are we—a fictional field that can be acted on, but one that is also hosting us and changing us as we inhabit it.

In the realm of cinema, "the fourth dimension" refers to the dimension of time. In spiritual practice, it can refer to the dimension of light—light not as the opposite of darkness, but light within darkness. Whenever one encounters a wall, or a space called darkness, one is not merely dealing with a finite boundary . . . the function of a wall or a boundary is not simply to stop you. It can also be to signal a departure and the possibility of a different presencing. So every time you hit a wall or an impasse, that

---

[1] The term film is deliberately used here, not because of a lack of differentiation between the two media (video and film), but because of the "bridge" digital technology has extended between them.

impasse can tell you a lot about yourself: having nowhere to go, you're "in"—at the beginning of something new that is happening.

For me, rituals (in Japanese culture and in digital technology for example), which concern one aspect of the film, delineate a very strong boundary defining the worlds of past and present, light and darkness, outsiders and insiders, or form and content. But when one really enters this boundary, really deals with it, it becomes a revolving door, something that opens both ways and allows you simultaneously entrance and exit. We can understand "the fourth dimension" in this sense. And, there is also a third meaning to "the fourth dimension": when some Japanese novelists use this term, it is usually to refer to that dimension of reality not immediately perceptible through "normal" sight. In other words, one has to lose one's "normal eye" in order to enter the fourth dimension.

V: *When you discussed the film after the screening, you were asked about representing tradition and Japanese rituals. You explained that you were not representing tradition as old and modernity as new. The film documents the dialectical relation between interrelated ideas of tradition and ideas of modernity. One dimension that is very present, even tangible, in your film is the mobility of the camera, by which you trace, in your own terms, this relation between two realms that are habitually conceived as separate. For example, at one point, the camera focuses on women dressed in traditional garb, and more particularly on the paraphernalia worn on the face, which looks like a gag, possibly because it was conceived as a way of constraining the woman and her voice. And yet, as the camera scrutinises, or rather, caresses the face of a woman, something comes through, in the woman's expression and in her eyes, in spite of the mask, or perhaps because of the mask, something that is unique to that woman.*

In this scene, as in many others, the camera performs a telescoping between ostensibly traditional custom and modern life, so that the woman's mask appears in an entirely new way. As you put it, it appears as a boundary that, as boundary, makes something new happen: here it produces the image of an individual woman in modern-day Japan. Could you say something about this "telescoping", and more particularly about the fact that such mobility does not so much stop but change at a specific moment in the film, so that half way through, the initial inventiveness—a very mobile camera, masked and split frames, sound de-spatialisation and an interesting use of the voice-over, which leaps, as it were, from voice-over to diegetic but off-screen voice and vice versa—turns into what seemed to me a more conventional, or perhaps just a more "well-behaved" mode of film-making. From that moment onward, the voice-over stabilises, even if it is still not the voice-over of conventional documentary film.

T: What new technology has always promised us is speed, portability, and mobility. Everything is going wireless—faster, smaller, and lighter. This is where tradition and modernity meet. Smallness, which remains an important quality of tradition, was what modernisation despised, as it equated prosperity and development with expansion in sise and in scale (bigger, taller, the more the better). What its grand-scale, universalising enterprise—and colonialism is here a grand example—sought to achieve was to make a clean sweep of all traditions and to raise everything anew from the ground. Today, in postmodern times, it is the return of smallness and portability that we're

witnessing, albeit a return that promotes not convivial tools but self-destruction at ever-faster speed. Guerrilla network and warfare in old and newly re-appropriated forms is the only way smaller nations have to fight the big powers. So mobility is, in effect, double-edged: the artificial return to the past via new technology may lead to further institutionalisation of individualism or it may contribute to new forms of decentralisation.

It seems most adequate to attack this problem in relation to Japan, a society whose genius often reveals itself in the way its creations—of old and new—manifest these values: maximum function, maximum productivity within minimal space and volume. Smallness and mobility characterise all aspects of cultural and economical life. This is why I turned to digital technology in visualising Japan. For me, the two are very linked. The mobility of the camera in *The Fourth Dimension* can be said to be effortless; literally, because I was using a small, very lightweight camera, and culturally, because of what I saw as prominent in Japanese aesthetics: the frame within the frame whose mobile, reflexive repetition, like the revolving door I mentioned earlier, encases and confines reality while it also allows infinity to come into view. It is through the finite, through the rituals of imaging (or of framing, scanning, panning, travelling and editing, for example) that infinity is made tangible. Devices suggestive of the mobility and multiplicity of framing are used throughout this digital film (more easily noticeable in the first part and last part), but as you've implied in your response, there's an important instance in its unfolding, which may bring about a shift in one's reception of the visual and aural material immediately following it.

There where the film takes on a "well-behaved" tone, to use your term, is when chronological time intervenes. In other words, the turning point in the film comes about with the evocation of Kamba Michiko's death.[2] In the midst of this fluid, multilayered time of travelling and image surfing, there's suddenly something like an arrest in the flow of events: without warning, the viewer confronts the linearity of a date ("May 19" then, "June 16, 1960"), the specificity of a proper name (Kamba Michiko), and the stillness of a face recaptured from a framed photograph. It is as if things have temporarily stopped in time or, as a statement in the film says, as if "time [were] frozen in its movement." This direct information on a political figure, this straight narrative of a historical event, or this representative arrest in the course of a film that otherwise makes no use of the conventional explicative mode of informing, is linked to what is being invoked on screen at that moment: a death. Albeit a death that tells of the *passing* of a historical epoch and its people. There is more than one way to make history. What seems important to me is to retain history's thickness and cultural dissemination in its unconcealed architecture. Here however, in the midst of that spatial thickness you suddenly have a linear temporality evolving with the single name and face of a woman.

I chose Kamba Michiko as the one political figure to evoke, precisely because of what I see as most representative in her death. With the struggle she led, her death may be said to have marked the turning point for the image the world had of Japan.

---

[2] Kamba Michiko was a student of Tokyo University and a well-known leader of the 20,000 Zengakuren students who demonstrated against the government of Prime Minister Kishi and the signing of the renewed Japan–U.S. Security Treaty.

Here, the emphasis is on *image*, since the film is not about (unmediated) Japan but about the image that one construes of Japan. Rather than trying to bypass its own reality as image, as time and light, the film deals with its production of "Japan's likeness." It is in this context that Kamba's death takes on its full significance as it tells us of a crucial passage in Japan's appearance: with the repression of a civic society, what was launched was a new image of Japan as a corporate society, for which the Western way became the way to progress. Given in a very straightforward manner, this historical information is then followed by a number of related statements, such as those on Japan's isolation from other Asian nations and on the lot of its immigrants—all selected for their contribution to Japan's image as a modern traditionalist society and a global economic power. By now, the viewer's ear is tuned to a different kind of narration, and the rest of the film can continue with a denser, accelerated rhythm between music, text, and image. The verbal fragments in voice-over are heard at much tighter intervals, while the visual returns, towards the end of the film, to some of the images presented at the beginning. Time is here being compressed; but the mobility of the camera remains.

V: *There is a wonderful image in the first half of the film: a long, panoramic shot of a Japanese torii gate in a lake and, behind it, skyscrapers. Slowly the camera moves out and down into the lake, with the shimmering waters reflecting the gate as well as the skyscrapers. The camera then closes in on the reflection, to show us its substance, as it were, that is, the many glistening streams of water and light that produce the reflection. It seemed to me a wonderful representation of history in all the density of the voices that constitute it. With the naming of Kamba Michiko, it is as if you arrested the camera to take a snapshot of that fluttering reflection. This does not mean that the water freezes: the glistening and the flowing continue, even if the snapshot is still. That is why, as you point out, the camera keeps on being mobile after the naming of Kamba Michiko, but in a different way. You are a multidisciplinary artist, but the interesting aspect of your activity, for me, is that, by being an artist and a cultural historian, you operate at the intersection of practice and theory. I wonder if the structure of* The Fourth Dimension, *the personal or subjective half and the historical or objective half, is related to this aspect of your work. And more generally, how do you handle the relation between practice and theory?*

T: I write poetry and theory, I teach and make film, and was trained as a musical composer. To many viewers, these are the strong dimensions in my films.

V: *Sound is indeed a very important aspect of* The Fourth Dimension, *not to mention music. I particularly appreciated the fact that in the film music has a visual as well as a sound dimension. I am thinking of the long and wonderful scenes showing drumming performances. First, during the ceremony, you show the men beating on very large, standing drums, the rhythm to which the women dance, dressed in traditional costume and wearing what looked like very painful wooden shoes. You then show the same ceremony with women at the drums. Next are a group of women drummers training: their bodies are immobile, only the arms move in impeccable synchronicity, while their faces, turned to the camera, are expressionless, in spite of their considerable effort involved in*

the exercise and the individual differences. The extent of their energy is conveyed by the potency of their music. You then cut to a street parade of bare-chested men drummers. In contrast to the women, their bodies are all over the place, they walk and jump in a disorderly manner, but their music is less potent; it does not hold the spectator in the same way because it is on a different narrative level. And then, to finish it off, you cut to a military parade, or, rather, a line-up of soldiers training in the street. They have their pants down, and, as the commander blows the whistle, they start dressing as fast they can. That was a wonderful sequence in which the music plays an important part, as music, sound, and visual performance. Or, again, in your use of the voice-over, which does not provide a comment of the image and which, moreover, leaps inside and outside the visual.

T: I am glad you mention the military sequence. You see, people talk about ritual as traditional, but the soldiers lining up to simulate an aspect of military training is a ritual that has nothing "traditional" about it, neither in the look nor in the action. It's rather hilarious when you think that of all possible representations of military bravery, it is that sequence which they choose to re-enact in the Sendai festival: sleeping with their underpants in a line on the street and competing in speed to regain a soldierly appearance at the sound of their commander's whistle—all of this carried out with *Star Wars'* grandiose music in the background. People apparently have no qualms inserting similar scenes in a festival which, like many other local festivals, is meant to reinforce social cohesion through tradition. The more one looks closely at these festival performances, the more one sees them as cultural hybrids and as meeting ground for the interaction of past, present, and future times.

The film abounds with examples of ritualised events that may have the look of tradition, but the action and performance of post-modernity, and vice-versa. I'm tempted here to say, who would do that but Japanese people? It's such a unique blend of utter conformity and odd liberty in both the revival and the modernisation of tradition. But the reality is that, whether we're Japanese or not, we all incorporate rituals and live by them in our everyday existence. Just look at rave culture (there's a sequence of it at the beginning of the film) or other youth cultures of our time: tribalism and its rituals are definitely part of this "new form of kindness," to use a statement in the film. Small and singular are what characterises the faces of resistance in the age of globalisation. Rather than seeing rituals only in terms of tradition and religion, it is interesting to widen the scope of our view and to expand the term to the daily activities of secular life.

To return to your question about theory and practice, there's a predominant tendency to see tradition as past and "timeless" and to equate modernism with the present and linear time—clock time or chronological time, for example. This is the way compartmentalised knowledge deals with reality: it can only speak in dualities and in pre-established hierarchies. Numbering our days, dating events, dividing, and counting as an end in itself seem to be the normative way of grappling with time. And yet, suffice it to say that time does not come in one unifying form; not only it exists in a multiplicity of forms and rhythms (biological, physiological, geological, and so on) at any single moment, it is also not limited to what humans can perceive. Time leaves traces in a multitude of layers and scales in the realm of life. Everything is time—stone, tree, mountain, ocean; thoughts, doubts, clouds—we are time. So it's absurd to talk about timelessness in this realm. You're "in time" when present and eternity meet. The "real" time—the one we tend not to see because we are caught up in it—is the "eternal present" that contains both past and future. This is how I would contextualise the relation between theory and practice in my work.

My activities as filmmaker, theorist, poet and composer, are tightly interwoven while they also constitute distinct, independent tracks. Making films or videos, composing with sound, writing and dicing with verbal language, each has its own unique reality to deal with. As I've been told, it is not uncommon that viewers of my films sometimes prefer, for example, to turn their attention primarily to the experience of hearing. They use a good sound system and just turn up the volume full blast, and they really enjoy listening to the musicality of the sound track, which can stand on its own, as do the visual and the verbal commentary, while being interwoven. You see, that's the notion of independence. Independence is not separation. It means to stand on one's own, independently, and yet relate.

I don't work with mere opposition. But, to some people's mind, it's still difficult to accept a relation of multiplicity without immediately turning it back into one of subordination and domination. For example, just look at what happens between the verbal and the visual or between sight and sound in both mainstream and alternative media. No wonder, from time to time, I encounter aggressions from viewers who, puzzled by the way I work through the question of politics in artistic realization and to offer a social view of the properties of an artistic medium, can only react negatively to the dynamics of theory and practice. Sometimes their questions may denote mere curiosity, which I welcome, other times they already imply a preconceived idea of what the practice of filmmaking should be, which is very stifling.

What bothers is the hearing eye, the image that hears what it says, looks at itself and tells of the instance of consumption while being consumed—the "pensive image" as Roland Barthes calls it, or the "boundary image" as I would prefer to put it. For the mainstream, theory and practice can only stand in mutual exclusion or submission: either your practice illustrates your theory, or your theory illustrates your practice. No independence.

If such logic is to prevail, then I would like to keep this question alive: which illustrates which? Is it theory or practice that comes first? It's like asking that consciousness be divided so that it can be fitted into the preconceived compartments of linear time, with a clear "before" and "after." Only people who don't really engage with theory would come up with the idea that a film can illustrate a theory and vice versa. It's funny, and I would challenge any filmmaker, "the best on the market" as they say, to do such a thing. Try as much as you wish, you can't make a film out of a theory. (One recognises immediately in montage, for example, that when an edit doesn't work, it's mainly because it is based on an idea.) Similarly, there is no theory that can entirely capture a practice. They are two different realities, each with its own light, its own precise workings. Always in excess, they escape one another. It is that challenge between the two that one keeps alive in the process of filmmaking.

If my inter- and multidisciplinary background is reflected in any way in my work, it is in the desire to maintain that independence among activities of production and among film elements. I don't remember having begun a film even with an idea; it has always been with a strong, mute feeling triggered by an encounter or by resonance

look at how long this fellow
has been sitting here:
our original face
has never been hidden

— Ko doja

between events; it's from there that everything happens. In "documentary" I don't work with a preconceived treatment or a well-outlined subject; and in "fiction," I write a very precise script with all the production details minutely indicated and drawn—but if the scenes are all there, they have no set order. They're like the pieces of a puzzle that will find their own order as the film takes shape. In both approaches, things come together through the process of shooting and editing, by putting yourself on the spot, as bound to a particular situation.

V: *What is interesting for me is that in doing so you document the process of "putting together things." I have seen many films that give this impression of fragmentation and immediacy. Especially work that uses digital technology. And yet, the majority conceal the process of "putting together things", the narrative, by erasing its marks. This is what is missing in a lot of digital work. There is a lot of fragmentation and pasting, but then the hand that fragments and pastes, the collating agent, is absent, or rather, is totally reified and presented as "technology", which leaves no margin for questioning the modalities of collation, the order of discourse. It is a kind of narrative that claims absolute power because, by compressing time and space, it allows no objection.*

T: I think you really put the finger on what largely goes unquestioned in new media works. When some programmers heard that I'd completed a digital video, they were extremely interested. But when they saw it, nothing of what I did quite fit into what they were expecting to see in digital "experimentation." The work, which fares in the grey zone of in-betweenness, often *seems* recognisable at first sight, although it remains with further sight "a non-recognisable entity" (a label that has been applied to both my artistic and scholarly works, and to myself). The kind of silent rejection with which it sometimes meets has mainly to do with what people perceive as "innovation": disturbances of the image that primarily, if not exclusively, involves the retina. Most of what has been priced in the field of digital visual production is limited to effects on the retina. All the other questions are taken for granted, such as the hand and brain that manipulate these effects, the social scope of art and technology, the politics of "forms" and of aesthetic decisions, in brief the question of the work's location and positioning.

The power at work and the cyborg's hand remain ultimately invisible. Digital effects that decompose and disintegrate the image abound in new media works and become an end in themselves. But how this process of returning to the void—to *no-image*—leads us further in understanding ourselves, the world of virtual reality and of datascapes, and the system that promotes this technology, does not seem to enter certain criteria for "innovation." In the reflexive play of my films, the space created to expose the making processes involved is not there for the mere sake of reflexivity—a notion whose significance is often taken in a very shallow way—but as a means to deconstruct the context in which we operate. And this is what affects us down to the smallest details of our lives. For example, the way we frame people tells not only about how and what we see, but also about the off-screen, the space excluded or not visible in the frame. *The Fourth Dimension* is said to open with a "panoramic" image: that image "on the move" (as differentiated from the "moving image") is at the same time a reference to the possibilities of filmmaking and to its limits. The focus is on both the literal and the figural limit of the image. I show this by offering a mobile re-framing, tracking the rectangle left and right, up and down, letting it trace its own boundary while hitting against the boundary of the screen frame.

V: *That is why I think your work is very interesting, and important. My students use the Internet, at times only the Internet, to do their research. When I tell them that the 'Net has to be used carefully, because some of the sources know less about cinema than the students themselves, they look surprised. Not because they are told that they know more than someone else, but because of my reminder of that "someone." It does not seem to enter into their heads that the material available on the 'Net is chosen (or not) and compiled by human beings.*

T: This attitude, which my film addresses, dwells on the persisting opposition between machine and humans. Of common acceptance is the belief that machines are objective and untainted by the subjectivity of human beings. This is all a question of boundaries. I am not aiming at achieving either one—objectivity or subjectivity. As discussed earlier, boundary breaching and crossing fosters new beginnings. In film and video, it is in the encounter of the organic and the technological that images of self and other are literally created. Like language, technology speaks of she (or he) who speaks it. We are captured in whatever we try to capture. What we face in this double co-existence is the two-times-two-ad-infinitum reality that regulates our everyday existence. We keep on thinking of objectivity and subjectivity as separate, but when the objectivity of a subjectivity comes into play or when a subjectivity within a subjectivity is set in motion, new horizons open up and we can deal with the relation differently.

This is also what I've brought out in *The Fourth Dimension*, with the exploration of machine time and human time in Japan's context of mobile forms and minute *care and control*. The modalities of such a mode of co-existence permeate every aspect of life, even the most mundane. For instance, in Europe, if you buy a train ticket and then decide to travel further than your ticket allows, you are immediately suspected of cheating and punished for your "misbehaviour" if you're caught. In Japan this is no problem: you pay a fare (the lowest if you wish) at the ticket machine so you can get on the train, then if you decide otherwise, you just wait for the conductor and pay the additional portion without anyone suspecting you in any way. Or, you can get on first class with a second-class ticket and pay the difference later; there's no wrongdoing when there's no distrust. It is a different relation to machine. Here, changing your mind, changing your itinerary at any moment in your journey does not make you look suspicious, because the system is not based, in this case, on the mutual exclusion of man and machine, but on their mutual co-operation. Instead of promoting competition, domination, and subordination, it emphasises the interactive and the collective in achievement. At another level, the same can be said of the relationship between tradition and modernity. Tradition is very present in Japan.

V: *But the same is true in European and generally in Western countries, even if their tradition can be, and often is, presented as very modern.*

T: Yes, it is hidden or denied even as it is carried on, whereas in Japan, whether peaceful or antagonistic, the co-existence of the two is put forward as an asset of the culture. This is what I gather from the struggle that many artists, architects, and writers from

Japan are carrying on in their works and in their desire to "synthesise the global and the particular" (their terms). And I'm saying this, despite the wide tendency in Japanese politics to equate Western with modern, to confuse "japanism" (the nostalgic flight to tradition) with "japaneseness," and hence, to reject, for the sake of modernisation, everything deemed to belong to "the past." A die-hard image that results from the perpetuation of this old divide between tradition and modernity is precisely the image of Japanese culture as an imported commodity, of Japanese creation as derivative—excelling only in imitation—and of Japanese spirit as fiercely xenophobic. Arguments from both the "ultra right" and the "ultra left" are based on such a partition. But what I find far more baffling or disquieting is the intimate pairing of care and control, the blurring of their differences in every aspect of the culture, which I strongly experience while living in Japan. What *The Fourth Dimension* offers then is an interval that allows one to work at shifting Japan's image, by focusing on the encounter while playing with these contested representations (which are narrow-minded but not false). With the current events of our times and with the on-going questions raised around the so-called "clash of civilisations," it is important to return anew to "tradition" and "modern," to question our normative sense of time, and to open to a more expansive and inclusive feel of "being-time."

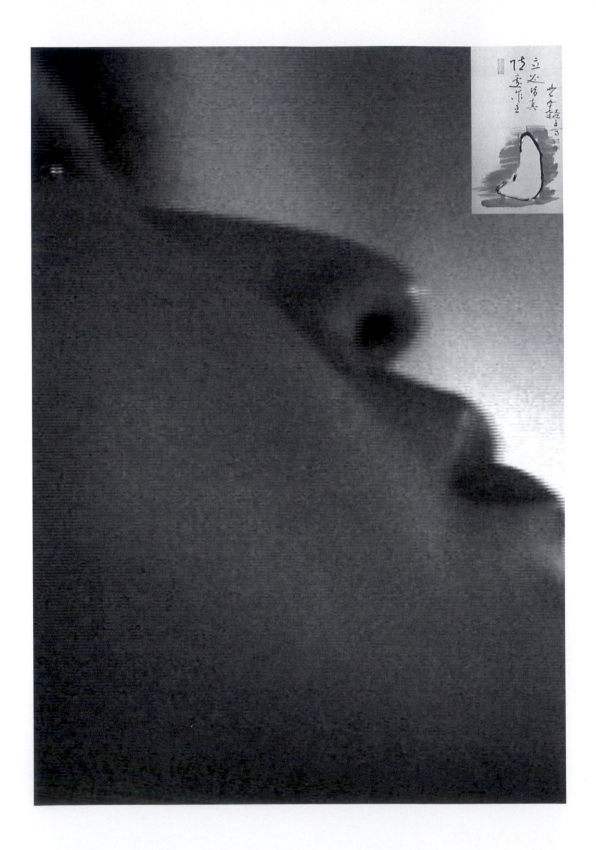

WHEN THE EYE FRAMES RED

with Akira Mizuta Lippit

First published in Japanese in *Intercommunications* (journal of art and technology, Tokyo, Japan), No 28, Spring 1999 (for part I); & No 29, Summer 1999 (for part II).

Lippit: *I want to begin by thanking you for agreeing to sit for this interview. It's perhaps worth noting that it is destined, at least in the first instance, for a Japanese audience. There has been a vibrant interest in your films and written work in Japan, where you have recently spent some time, so perhaps we can touch upon those experiences and your reception there a little later.*

It is in some ways an extremely difficult task to approach you for an interview. The conventions of this medium assume some notion of a constant or discernable identity, an interviewee whose essential features are either already known or can be known. In the case of Trinh T. Minh-ha, one recognizes a filmmaker and a scholar, but also an artist of many shades, a perpetual traveler, and a person whose own history in the world is marked by the epistemic shifts that characterize this century and its thought. Looking back on the various interviews collected in Framer Framed, *I'm struck by the sheer diversity of subjects that you speak of, but also by the sometimes anxious ways in which the interviewer tries, at times, to situate you within established traditions of experimental filmmaking, the critique of anthropology and conventional documentary, ethnography, poetics, post-colonial thought, feminist thought and activity, and so forth. I'll try to resist the temptation to identify, as it were, a fixed dwelling and try instead to follow the nomadic qualities of your expansive work.*

Since many of your previous interviews speak to your cultural politics and positions vis-à-vis the subject of alterity, I thought we might approach this conversation from the vantage of your films, which represent, in my opinion, absolutely discrete and distinct pieces of work that are nonetheless bound by a very particular spirit or desire. So, perhaps to begin with this notion of a project, how do you define your film project—if you accept the notion of a project—and how does your film work fit into your broader artistic and intellectual projects?

Trinh: When I work on a film, I am drawn very intensely to the world of images and sounds. On a basic level, such a state of creative availability and of active receptivity is in itself a "project." But the making of a film also opens up many doors to other means of creativity. It sharpens the edge between, let's say, writing for a book and writing for a film—a difference one constantly faces when words are part of the film fabric. Not only does the use of language differ markedly from one medium to another, but working with storytelling, poetry, and everyday speech in cinema also makes me aware of music in ways I never thought of before. If a poem is an invisible painting, as Chinese artists put it, then a film can be all at once visible poetry, musical painting, and pictorial music. The spaces between image, sound, and text remain spaces of generative multiplicity, in which the function of each is not to serve nor to rule over the other, but to expose, in their tight interactions, each other's limit. What I cannot avoid experiencing at certain moments of the process is both the different strengths and limits of these tools of creativity. So it is in working constantly with these limits and with the circumstances that define them that I advance—quite blindly, actually. Even though, in discussions, it does seem as if all my projects are very lucidly thought out, this comes in the making process, not before it. Most of the time I jump into a project blindly, and this is how boundaries are also displaced.

L: *So you see the production of a film as something that opens up a space for writing, thinking, and learning, even as you are creating the work itself?*

T: Yes, very strongly. There's a whole web of activities involved in and triggered by the making of cinematic images. I have no such thing as a preconceived idea that I want to visualize or illustrate through film. It doesn't happen that way; it's more likely through an encounter—with a person, with a group of people, with an event, or with a current of energy that is sparked by a specific situation.

L: *Your body of films suggests a certain consistency, an idea not of any totality, but of a shared quality. When thinking in the abstract about your films, they seem to offer a shape, to have and take shape, yet when one looks at the films individually, they are in many ways radically different. There persists, however, a common desire or spirit that motivates them. One motif that appears strongly in all your work involves an aesthetic or politics of travel. Another is the notion of encounter and portraiture, a portraiture that is not always of people or places but sometimes of relations to places, producing a sense in which the viewer finds herself or himself the subject of a portrait—as if the spectator is being watched.*

I am interested in this dual sense of absolutely discrete projects with completely separate foci and emphases on the one hand, and the persistence of a communal space that works in your films on the other. I have noticed that interviewers often try to identify you within very specific communities, and it seems impossible to do so. There is, it seems, something fundamentally nomadic about your work both in its geographical momentum but also in its intellectual or creative capacity to wander, as it were, and move.

T: Perhaps something that seems recognizable in my work and can only be realized intuitively with each film, is this tendency in pushing the limits, to lead the work, just when its structure emerges, to the very edge where its potential to return to nothing also becomes tangible. Whatever takes shape does not do so simply in order to address form. In that sense, nothing really takes shape. By going toward things while letting them come to me in the mutually transformative process of filmmaking, I am not merely "giving form." Taking shape is not a moment of arrival, and the question is not that of bringing something vague into visibility. Rather, the coming into shape is always a way to address the fact that there is no shape. Form is here an instance of formlessness, and vice versa.

So when you talk about this sense of traveling, of wandering, and of not fitting comfortably in one group, it's not so much something that constitutes an agenda on my part as something rather intuitive that corresponds to the way I live, to the skills of survival I've had to develop, and to my own sense of identity. I'm not at all interested in giving form to the formless, which is often what many creators reach for. Rather, I'm taken in by the creative process through which the form attained acutely speaks to the fragile and infinite reality of the world of forms—or, of living and dying.

How to incorporate that sense of the infinite in film is most exciting, even though we know that we always need a beginning and an ending, and that making a film is already to stop the flow or to offer a form. But rather than reaching a point of completion where form closes down on form, a closure can act simultaneously as an opening when it addresses the impossibility of framing reality in its subtle mobility. This is certainly one way of looking at what happens with all of my films.

The other aspect you mentioned, which I love very much, is that, yes, there is a tendency to see the two films I shot in Africa as being alike, and sometimes they are even scheduled to be screened one after the other in the same program slot. This is a terrible mistake, for *Reassemblage* and *Naked Spaces* need to be viewed as far apart from one another as possible, if the spectator's creative and critical ability is to be solicited. Such a programming decision, detrimental to the reception of the films, tells us how people continue to see films predominantly in terms of subject matter. Yet how the two films are realized and how they physically affect the viewer are radically different. As I mentioned earlier, each encounter is so utterly bound to the elements that define it, that for me it is impossible to reproduce, identically, what has been made at different moments of one's itinerary, and with different peoples, circumstances, and locations. The specificity of each encounter would dictate a different move for each film. In other words, each film has its own . . . field of energies.

L: *Yes, a vitality. It is surprising to think of* Reassemblage *and* Naked Spaces *as similar films. Do you feel that sometimes because the subject matter can be so powerful in your work that it interferes or disrupts other elements in the work? The subject matter you select is often very powerful.*

T: I'm very glad it comes out that way for you. There's always a tendency to think that because I don't come into a project with an idea in mind or with a preconceived political agenda, the content is of little account, which is not at all the case. I feel very strongly about the subject matter of each of the films—again, not as something that precedes, but something that comes with the making of these films. In fact, people bewildered by the freedom with which my films are structured often react by saying, "Well then this film could have been made anywhere." And I would have to say "No," because each film generates its own bodyscape—as related to specific places, movements, events, and peoples—which cannot be reproduced elsewhere.

But yes, I would agree that if the subject matter comes out strongly, then what we call structure, form, or even process, become less noticeable. Not because they are in any way less important, but because when everything clicks together in a film, it's no longer possible to speak of form and content as separate entities. This reminds me of the other dimension, which you touched on earlier, namely, that the subject who films is always caught in the process of relating—or of making and re-presenting—and is not to be found outside that process. All of my films are actually attempts to bring out that process with and within the image. Because of the very tight "always-in-relation-to" situation, it is also difficult to simply indulge in the subject matter, as if it pre-exists out there, waiting to be retrieved "as it is." There should always be some kind of a split somewhere that compels the viewer to pull out of the illusory screen space where subject matter tends to take over film reality.

L: *In watching your films again recently, but also following from what you have just spoken of, I am interested in your sense of framing. It has a peculiar tendency, although different from film to film, to make the familiar look unfamiliar, even peculiar and unknown. I am thinking especially of* Reassemblage, *where one looks at images that are part of a cultural vocabulary and yet the look of that film is so absolutely distinct that one begins to notice the very consistent but subtle sense of framing. Perhaps that also relates to your earlier comments about edges and borders. The framing doesn't operate according to conventions, to the demands of balance or symmetry. Could you speak of your ideas regarding framing?*

T: Yes, actually we can go in many directions with this because it reminds me that when *Reassemblage* was first released, there were often, unavoidably, a couple of viewers in the audience at each screening who either praised the film or got very upset because they related it to a *National Geographic* product. Even today, I still occasionally encounter those kinds of responses, whether in the U.S., in Europe, or in Asia. And of course, there have also been instances where there is someone in the room who works for National Geographic who immediately says, "We would never accept such a film."

Sometimes the mere fact that the subject matter is located in rural contexts or in remote parts of the non-Western world (what the Japanese film milieu commonly calls "ethnic films"), and the fact that, in addition, the images are bright and colorful, with no immediately definable or recognizable political agenda attached, are sufficient for some viewers to attribute the film's look to the more familiar one of *National Geographic* images. I once said in response to a similar, aggressively voiced reaction that, ah yes, for some people all reds look alike, and that for them there's no difference between the red of a rose, the red of a ruby and the red of a flag; nor is there any difference within the reds of blood flowing unseen in life and of blood spilled out conspicuously in death.

Fortunately, a number of viewers do come to acknowledge on their own that what they first thought of as a *National Geographic*-type film does work on them, as the film advances, in such a way as to leave them ultimately perplexed and troubled. Days and even weeks after, they say, their perceptions of the film continue subtly to expand and

to open onto unexpected views and directions. For me, this is largely due to a process of shooting and framing in which, as I mentioned earlier, the filming subject and the filming tools are always caught in the subject filmed. I don't mind it when viewers in Europe link my films to those of Johan Van der Keuken, who is known as one of those truly "mad about framing." I am not so much concerned here with composition, but as you've noted, I'm sensitive to the borders, edges and margins of an image—not only in terms of its rectangular confines, which today's digital technology easily modifies, but in the wider sense of framing as an intrinsic activity of image-making and of relation-forming. Working with Jean-Paul Bourdier, who is an architect, has incited me to see in terms of space so as to decide where to put the camera and how to move with it. This is quite prominent in *A Tale of Love*, for example. *Reassemblage* and a large part of *Naked Spaces* were shot intuitively with the camera placed very close to ground level, where most daily activities are carried out in African villages. Such a decision has an important impact on the image, but the frame itself is very intimately created while I am shooting.

Most of the time, if a good cinematographer sees an interesting subject and wants to use a pan, for example, she rehearses the gesture until the movement effected from one object to another is impeccable in its precision and certainty. In my case, I usually shoot with no forepractice and often with only one eye—the kino-eye, as Vertov called it. I may at times shoot the same subject more than once, but well, the first time always turns out to be the best, because when one repeats the gesture one becomes sure of oneself, which is what most cinematographers value—the sureness and smoothness of the gesture. But what I value is the hesitation or whatever happens when I first encounter what I am seeing through the camera lens. So the way one looks becomes totally unpredictable. Like wearing blinders and not seeing where one is going, the camera just moves with you according to the pace of your own body, or the pace of your camera pan. It is this attentive half-blindness that interests me. Rather than merely conforming to the ideal of seeing with both eyes while shooting—one inside, the other outside the lens and the frame so as to foresee one's moves—I largely confine myself in the films I've shot to the eye that only sees reality via the camera. There is, in the look that goes toward things while letting things come to it unplanned, no desire to capture per se. You start a move and then simply continue it to see what comes into that framing in time and space.

Now there are films where I've worked with a cameraperson because I had to do more directing. Here, it is difficult to talk about one approach, because mine is necessarily mediated by the camera operator. In *Surname Viet Given Name Nam*, in the interview scenes of *Shoot for the Contents*, and especially in *A Tale of Love* where fiction intensifies framing, the sureness of the cinematographer's hand is inevitable. But I value that element as well when it doesn't come from me. For it is then simply another element that contributes to the experience of film as an activity of production. Non-knowingness is an attitude, not a technique to perform. What is specific to the cinematographer also has a place, and even if that cinematographer does not decide on the framing, the gesture, rhythm, and sureness developed are hers. Treating these as her contribution to the process also means that one necessarily creates a different space for the film. What you have is something, let's say, between the open-ended process of the filmmaker and the skilled expertise of the operator.

L: *The images are beautiful in your films, strikingly beautiful—much more so than in National Geographic—and that may be an effect precisely of what you have described. Your description of the process of filmmaking for you suggests something more on the order of the sublime. Rather positing mastery over her medium, her subject matter, the filmmaker here loses herself in the process of making a film. It's very different from the more popular notion of the filmmaker as a master of one's craft, of one's subject, of one's space. Your description of the first gesture, the first movement as the one that you regularly prefer suggests a kind of dissipation or a loss of the self in the act of filmmaking. And the result can be a very beautiful image that emerges from the encounter with that dissipation, rather than from the assertion of one's mastery in the form of a pan, or tilt, or some kind of practiced gesture.*

T: What you've just elucidated is very different from how people usually understand it. I feel much more affinity with the terms you use—"the loss of oneself," by which one gains everything else, and hence no mere loss. The tendency among many, when I try to put this process of filmmaking into words, is immediately to recast it in terms of spontaneity and personal subjectivity. The first gesture is then viewed as the more truthful one. But the moment of spontaneity, which is so sacred for modernist art in general, has its limits. One can be quite clichéd when being spontaneous. And there are often more instances, where instead of encountering elements of surprise or newness in spontaneity, one simply faces a form of reification of the individualist self.

L: *The fantasy of a spontaneous gesture does suggest the emergence of an authentic or genuine self, a truer self that escapes in the inattention of spontaneity. Another feature that I find striking in your work is the adamant tension between images, but also the sounds that are sometimes naturalistic and at others synthetic, artificial, and staged. Sounds are often broken, just when one is ready to be drawn into their flow. And one feels this at work in a variety of places, certainly I would say in* Shoot for the Contents. *During the interview with the Chinese filmmaker, for example, one recognizes a very theatrical mise-en-scene—similarly in the interviews that constitute* Surname Viet Given Name Nam. *Do you see these tensions between naturalistic and synthetic representations as an element of your style, or do you see them as a dialectic that works between the notion of nature, naturalism, or things as they are, and the process of reflecting, commenting, filmmaking—"being nearby"?*

T: Neither one of those. Perhaps if I can find a way to say it on my own terms, it would be to say that what is viewed as being natural on the one hand and staged on the other belongs to a whole process. If one looks at the image in terms of representation, then I'm not simply representing "substance," but I'm actually bringing out what one can call "function" or "condition." In *Shoot for the Contents*, the image is mediated by the translator—a literal translator during the interview with the Chinese filmmaker, but also other translators heard or seen through the voices of the narrators and of myself as writer, editor and photographer of images of China. The fact that both makers and viewers depend here on translation in order to have an "entry" into the culture was clearly brought out in the sound-image. On one level, this interdependence made visible and audible may appear artificial, but on the level of its function within the process of producing meaning, and images, it is totally natural.

This "natural" process is precisely what has been widely suppressed in films that try to get at "substance" while forgetting the importance of function and field in the mediation of reality on film. As the Indian philosopher Coomaraswami said, one cannot imitate nature, one can only operate the way nature operates. When one thinks in those terms, the two currents you mentioned (one naturalistic, the other synthetic) are one and the same. To call attention to the subjectivity at work and to show the activity of production in the production is to deal with film in its most natural, realistic, and truthful aspect. So I don't see the separation. This largely applies to my first four films; with *A Tale of Love*, where everything was thought out down to the smallest detail, the situation is different. Ultimately, despite the contrasting way with which this last film fractures conventions of genre and of narrativity—or of psychological realism in acting and in consuming—its direction expands the one adopted by the previous films.

L: *In* A Tale of Love, *I was struck by, among other things, your use of colors and filters, which reminded me of the beginning of* Naked Spaces, *where you use a very saturated, seemingly tinted image. It creates a disorienting space because the colors and textures are so vibrant and voluptuous throughout the film that one begins to distrust one's own senses. One can no longer tell what the so-called real colors of a scene are and those colors begin to infuse more than just the image, but all of one's perceptions, projections, fantasies. It produces a kind of hybrid space, fantastic and actual. This coloring also seems to operate in* A Tale of Love, *which replays a previous tale,* The Tale of Kieu, *not as a historical citation, but as something that forms a hybrid text between a historical document and one's interpretations of it. You make this clear in the film and in an encounter I saw you have with a member the audience at a screening of* A Tale of Love. *She was an older Vietnamese woman who insisted that* A Tale of Love *was very different from the text she had studied in school. It seemed to be a perfect response to the film precisely because you suggest that there are always these hybrids that are forming between an external space grounded in reality and one's encounter with it, which immediately creates some sort of space in between. Could you talk about your own motivation in* A Tale of Love *and the kind of interest that drew you to that project?*

T: There are actually two things in your response that I would love to discuss. First, I find it very interesting that you link the two films through color. Second, I would come back to the twist you've brought out, which turns the Vietnamese woman's negative response into an accurate response for the space created. Other members of the Vietnamese community who have seen the film have also given a number of very interesting reactions. For example, the epigraph seen on screen at the beginning of the film is a quotation of the ending lines of the 3254-verse poem. So "Why begin with the ending?" some asked and added, "Not only that, but afterwards, you enter the poem in such diverse places that it throws us off and we are confused." One man told me, however, that because of these decisive cuts into the different parts of the poem, he saw through the film, the space between makers and characters. This was wonderful for me, even though he didn't mean it in a positive way and was telling me about this undesirable split in which "your character is timorous and undecided but you are a very tough person."

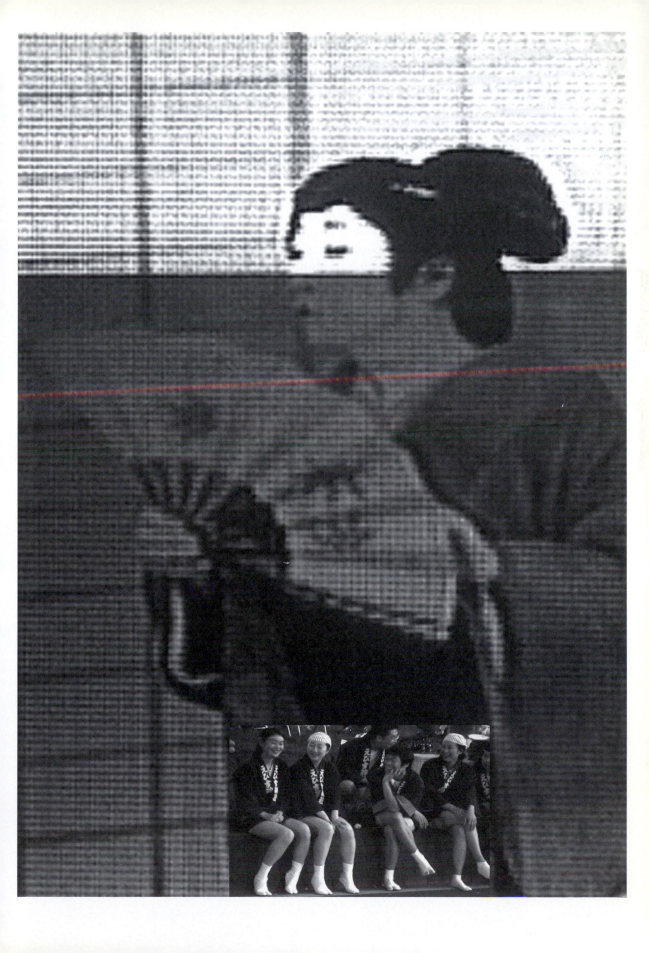

In the context of patriarchal Vietnamese culture, this was no praise at all. But then I was very curious and I asked more specifically why he thought so. He said the way I edited the film was such that every time he started settling in with a recognizable thread of the poem, the cuts again and again jerked him out of the story space. He saw in the edits what one can call the split of voices, which is an interesting reaction when compared to the tendency among Western audiences to identify the filmmaker with the main character. The question asked often revolves around whether the film tells of a personal experience. "Does this come from your personal life?" It makes things very difficult because certainly, I would have been totally unable to make a film if it hadn't engaged me strongly in a personal way, but this has little to do with one's own particular life. It would be of no interest if filmmaking and film viewing merely invited identification rather than offered an encounter with what is larger than one's individual self—that is, with one's own spaciousness.

To come back to the question of color, the tinted effect of that very first sequence of images in *Naked Spaces* actually comes from a rather "natural" process. The Kodak film stock we carried with much care with us over a period of nine months of travel across West Africa was, in general, quite reliable. But perhaps the heat played a role here, because amidst all this footage of accurate colors, we suddenly found two rolls that came out all red. When I called the lab to ask what had happened, nobody understood why it had come out that red—because it could have turned out slightly tinted, brownish or partly reddish, which is the usual case with older film stock. I was actually quite happy with the look, and since I didn't cause this effect on purpose, I immediately saw it as part of this solicited "otherness" in filming.

One of the film's foci was the wall paintings of African dwellings, whose colors change with our perception and with the shift of light through the day. Light and darkness also structure people's living spaces and influence women's daily activities. There is a whole network of relationships built up in *Naked Spaces* between film, music, architecture, and social life through elements such as light, color and sound. So the red incidentally caused by the heat appears as a natural process that easily finds its place in the main threads of the film. But by opening the film with this red sequence, I'm also using the color as a marker to invite the viewer to come into the film differently—with a light that can pull you far in, as differentiated from the green that pulls you out in the subsequent images; and a light by which you are projected into another state of mind even while you look at things "as they are." When you encounter colors in such a state, as you so nicely put it, the dualism of inside and outside loses its pertinence; you are no longer so sure of how colors come to you, from in here or from out there. This is also how I see those houses: as you stay with a space and try to shoot it at different times of the day, you can see how light and colors are shifting in ways that open onto an inner landscape unseen by your daily purblind eyes.

In *A Tale of Love*, the question of color is almost the opposite: you create it as an explicit part of lighting. Since we had to plan out all the details in a "narrative film," with a large crew shooting from a script, we were dealing with a very constraining space. How is one to conceive of lighting when it is not simply used to fill in a space, to make things legible, to hierarchize and to dramatize according to psychological realism? By visualizing it, for example, in terms not only of projection but also of absorption. The move here is to experience light as it is formed by the differing qualities of darkness and by the receptive properties of things (texture, tone, movement, reflective potential) in relation to their surrounding. Here, color (as an attribute of life in *Naked Spaces*) comes in as one of the ways by which light itself takes shape. Just as the primary colors featured in the film stand on their own in a challenging relationship of multiplicity (rather than of complementarity), many of the lights that cross the frame have a distinct shape and color of their own. We might say then, to use a term we discussed earlier, that this space in *A Tale of Love* is saturated with artificiality; which is fine with me because it's what the making of a film with a script should acknowledge—a space carefully fabricated, if not entirely fabulated. But again, "artificial" is not opposed to "real" or "true," for to materialize a reality, one has to resort to the "non-true," and it is finally through the fictional—be it image or word—that truth is addressed.

L: *The story of color in* Naked Spaces *is quite fascinating. It is as if the place, or the process, as heat had pressed itself onto the film directly, creating a tactile trace of its having been touched—a fortuitous disaster it seems. In a similar vein, I know you have discussed in the past your relationship to the interval, to uses of silence, or a variation of silence, speechlessness, which comes up as a motif in a number of your works. I am interested in not only the intervals of sound or silence that appear on your soundtracks, but the ways in which one feels those intervals or silences even when there is sound. Which is to say that the exploration of intervals or silence in your work seems to be at such a sophisticated level that it occurs even when it isn't, strictly speaking, a moment of silence or pause, or some interruption of the sound. I was wondering if you could situate your interest in the concept of silence, and how it works in relation to your work, which is also very discursive.*

T: When I discuss my work with an audience, what I generate from their reception of the film is something different from the film. I can't tell them what "the film is all about" (which is what film reviewers often claim to do), for I do not wish to imitate what the film is doing. Rather, what I try to give to the audience is yet another space with the film. Very often discussants tend to confuse this discursive verbal space with the film and say, "it's so complex, how can people who haven't heard you understand the film?" But film and discussion are two different realities. Aside from the fact that you can't assume that nobody understands because you don't understand, "understanding" also cannot account for the whole of film experience; it is only one among the many other possible activities of reception. Once, in a public discussion of my work, a viewer made a very complicated and long-winded remark that ended disapprovingly with this statement: "Art should be simple." And I agree. Even when the opinion comes from someone who can't be simple in his response. Simplicity has always been a big challenge for artists. But the simplicity of a film has little to do with the complex responses it can generate. The simplest work tends to yield the widest range of readings and of critical thinking. Simplicity and complexity, as it is stated several times in *Naked Spaces*, really go together.

Similarly, silence expresses itself in many ways and can be said to be a whole language of its own. Sometimes speaking is a way of keeping silence and being silent is an effective way of speaking. This is often the case in repressed political contexts, such as for example the case of the calligrapher who appeared on screen toward the end of *Shoot for the Contents*, and whose answer to the question, "Why did you move from Shanghai?" was so clearly a form of silence, that I decided the best way to translate it, was not to translate. This moment of non-translation in a film that directly addresses the issue of translation has raised questions among a lot of people.

As you said, silence can be a moment when you don't hear sound and this can be radically disturbing when taken literally. In film, silence usually means filling the soundtrack with discreet environmental sound like birds singing or water lapping, or else with what is technically called "room tone." In *Reassemblage* I actually cut off all sound from time to time, creating this dreadful phenomenon for filmmakers known as sound holes. A very perceptive viewer told me that when he saw *Reassemblage*, because of the way that the soundtrack was cut off, he suddenly had glimpses of a spectral reality that addressed him directly. He said that it was an experience of death irrupting between images and in a way, he's an ideal viewer for that film. Rather than simply equating a sound hole with a technical mistake, one can ask what effect this has on the viewer, what reality is brought about? The reality of something we call death, or among others, the reality of the room in which the film is showing—the snoring of the audience, the squeaking of seats, the noise of the projector or the pulsation of one's own body, as Cage musically experienced it.

It's very difficult to simply talk about silence as a homogeneous phenomenon. As you've noticed, even when there's sound or a lot of talking, you can still feel that interval. I really appreciate that, because, unlike with the films shot in Africa, *Surname Viet Given Name Nam*, *Shoot for the Contents* and *A Tale of Love* feature language in its excess as it outdoes the will to speak and to mean. There are also moments when words become nonsense, which is another aspect of language that I often work with humorously. After so much speech, you come to a state where opposites really meet. You may say or hear one thing but you're supposed to mean or to understand exactly the opposite, which was the case with such terms as left and right, right and wrong, as related to China's politics. But that's the nature of language. When one pushes it far enough, words start to mingle, they are no longer opposites and the more one goes into it, the more one sees how these words used excessively can also silently open up a critical space.

L: *What I find especially liberating in your films is the way in which you track the movement of language from a place to its destination. And frequently, it doesn't arrive at its destination, which is a much more compelling way of thinking about language, communication, all of the complexities of its transmission, and translation. That non-arrival, or missed arrival seems much more provocative and much more familiar, even, as an experience than the shot/reverse-shot convention in which movie conversations are usually sent and received. In another interview, you relate the experience of a translator running up to you frantically and saying "But there are two voices here, which one do we translate?" The fact that things are lost or miscommunicated or fail to arrive at their destinations is hardly frustrating, but actually a relief to see in film, because it really begins to address the circuitry of language. It seems that in your films the interview is never a stable phenomenon, even from film to film, but something that is addressed and created as*

a space each time anew, never occurring in the same way. Each space seems to be driven or motivated by the particularities of that space and your relationship to it.

T: If people thought about language in the way you just described it, then my films are very simple. It's the same with my books. I do hear from a number of academics that my books are very difficult. And I don't deny this. On the other hand, I've also met people who left school at the age of fifteen or who have no training for theoretical thought. They come across these books by accident and they can't read many pages in one go, but they have no concern for that, they just steadily read a few pages at a time and say it's incredible, because they feel a lot of affinity with the process of my thought and can follow it so well. If one simply observes how language operates—creating all these circuits within itself, as you said—and how it works on us constantly, then these films are very easy to "understand."

When an interview is dense and intense, as in the case of those in *Surname Viet Given Name Nam*, then even in moments when one is not in front of the interviewee, the conversation continues, not in one voice, but sometimes in several voices, or in fragments that come and go and get superimposed on one another. There's nothing difficult in the film when one thinks inclusively in terms of what language does to us—how it speaks us as we speak it—rather than exclusively in terms of ourselves as the ones who manipulate language. Any one of those instances that may irritate the viewer by its so-called incomprehensibility is for me as clear as a river. They happen all the time in our daily reality with language.

Regarding the anecdote about which voice to translate when there are several simultaneous voices, I was amazed by the Japanese solution. Actually, with Japanese characters, that problem did not even arise; my distributor at Image Forum simply decided to have one voice subtitled vertically, the other, horizontally. Not only do calligraphic characters destroy the image much less, but you also have this flexibility of going vertical or horizontal.

L: *When* A Tale of Love *was about to be released there was a small fervor that Trinh T. Minh-ha had made a narrative film, and there was something of a scent of scandal about the whole thing. When I heard this rumor, I was a little surprised because it is not as if your previous films could be classified as strictly non-narrative work either. They had elements or traces of things that one might call documentary, for example, or experimental or art film, or music film. And then when I saw* A Tale of Love *I was reassured that this wasn't a narrative in the way that people seemed to be disparaging the term either. Certainly it was a narrative and it engaged aspects of narrative. But it was also done in 35mm. Could you talk about your decision to work with this format and this narrative structure? What prompted you to explore this particular set of elements?*

T: It's just like with the color red discussed earlier in Naked Spaces. The decision was bound to circumstances. I didn't have the budget to shoot a "feature narrative film," not even a budget for 16 mm. So in a desperate move, the line producer called everywhere searching for donations. Panavision donated the camera equipment in 35mm for the whole shoot, rather than in 16mm as we had asked, which was such an incredible thing. But I paid dearly for that, because I got stuck after the film was finished. The final edited version was completed in 1995 but I had to wait until 1996 before the film could be released in an acceptable form because there was no money left to make a print.

Certainly, there's also another decision that comes into play. And as you said, it's not so much a question of narrative versus documentary, it's more a question of exploring a different terrain of cinema. Since I've explored at length the terrain of, let's say, information and truth, I wanted to explore this other terrain which is that of the lie and its truth in love stories. I wanted to see what happens when you deal with something as commonly consumed in our society as the love story. But as you can see, despite the difference in realization, the direction explored is similar to the one taken in the previous films.

L: *In each of your films, one senses the particularity of a place and a space that seems to orient the film. One feels that the space is dictating or directing the movements of the film, a mixing of geography and fantasy, experience and projection. Knowing that you have spent some time in Japan recently, and that you are also working on a new project, I was wondering if you could talk about your new project and also about your sense of Japanese space?*

T: It's difficult to talk about a visual space before you get a chance to see it realized on film or video. I've just only started work on it, but let's say that after having been to Japan, I think, five times, my experience of the culture during this last four-month stay, which was the longest stay, has changed quite a bit. It was a thoroughly demystifying experience, although not in a negative sense. You just have a reality that is differently nuanced, less romantic, but also less exotically other.

As with many foreigners, I am drawn to the spiritually ritualized aspects of Japanese life and art. The integrated dimension of aesthetics and ethics has been quite striking in a number of Japanese works, for example. I am very attracted to shooting in Japan partly because of its architectural landscape, which really favors the graphic line and the mobility of sliding frames. Here, the line between outside and inside is always shifting. It seems as if everything—from the art of building houses to the way the railroad network functions, or the way dance and music structure theatrical performances and festival parades—partakes in a system whose organization is largely based on micro-structures or on prefabricated cells (the melodic, the rhythmic, the action-propelling and the structure-bearing cells in a parade, for example). There's also a striking encounter between light, color, and graphics in the scenography of life and stage events that I would love to work with. But as always, I have to remain very flexible as to what I can do, since I don't work with unlimited finances and everything still depends very much on that. I have to take into consideration the fact that maybe I will not be able to get permission for the locations where I would love to shoot, such as in temples, since the next film is very much related to a spiritual quest.

At the end of this millennium the notion of spirituality may continue to raise skepticism because what is spiritual is often identified, at least in the modern world, with mystification and institutionalized religion. A return to the traditions of old is also to be rejected as long as these are viewed only through activities of retrieval and of imitation rather than of creation in the present. This, I think, is the very problem we face today, both in the modern East and in the West, with our inability to see the spiritual

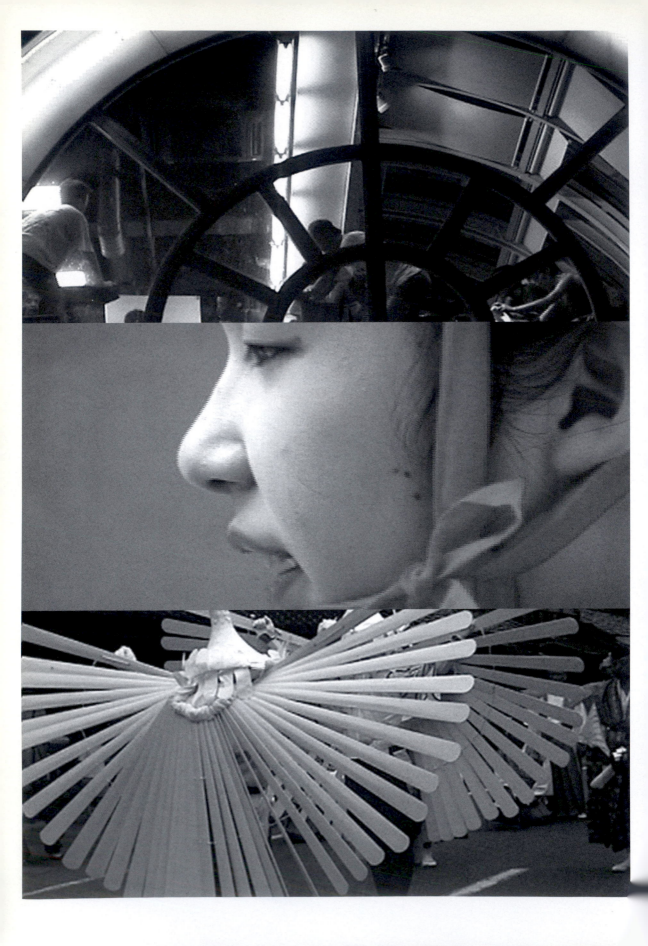

in any other way than smugly and narrow-mindedly, as a form of parasitical occultism and of transcendentalism. The situations with Tibet or with Islam are glaring examples. As a spiritual force that gathers people across geographies and nations, Islam certainly stands, despite all controversies, as the one visible power that continues to challenge the West at the end of the millennium. It is necessary in these times to look at spirituality in a different way. And certainly, Japan has had a strong tradition of writers and filmmakers who have struggled with this dimension of life, from which I also draw inspiration.

L: *These glimpses are very intriguing. The quest for a spiritual existence or identity, a rethinking of spirituality, should be of interest to late-capitalist Japan as well. Thank you very much.*

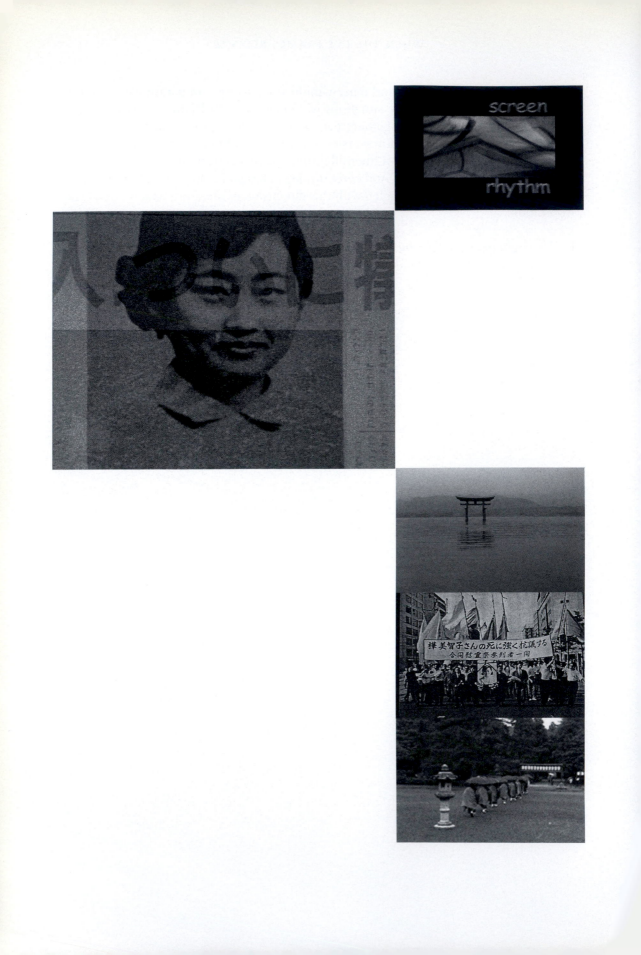

TIME PATHS

with Lynn Marie Kirby

This is a shortened version of the dialogue "Time Paths" first published in the monograph *Discrete and Continuous Boundary Problems,* on the occasion of Kirby's 2002 San Francisco Cinematheque retrospective.

Trinh: *Perhaps we can begin with the work that you are doing now, since you are going to have a retrospective in the fall (2002).*

Kirby: I'm going to be doing three nights of programs that I'm calling "Discrete and Continuous Boundary Problems." The shows include a selection of recent and older films and videos, with an installation or performance each evening. One of the newest pieces I am planning to show is *In Search of the Baths of Constantine.* We've had conversations about this improvisational way of editing and the idea of whether the time of the performance is sacred. Here it was important that what I digitized into the computer, the original gesture in time, maintain its integrity. In other words the meaning of the piece had to come from dilating the time within a particular moment rather than through the editing of images in time.

   In Search of the Baths of Constantine was the first piece that I did scrubbing live in the timeline. As the image is outputting to tape, I move back and forth in time. Not only was I working with the time of my movement through the timeline, but also I was actually working with the hard disk inside the computer. The mechanism of the disks themselves controlled my movement. Depending on how much material I would have on the hard disk, I could move slower or faster through the timeline. There is an invisible hardware partner that I was in conversation with—inside the computer. This is in contrast to DJ's who work with vinyl, who see where they're going on the disk.

   You came to the studio when I began this work and I showed you the work in progress. We were discussing how it breathed in time, and it did seem like there was something missing, but I would not allow myself to go into the gesture to edit. I realized that the presentation form needed to be an installation that could express both linear and cyclical time. I wanted to work with the idea that time has a linear form in the theatrical space. We walk into a theatrical space with an anticipation of a beginning and an end. We sit in the dark. One of the things that I love about film-making is that one can capture people in the dark. Yet I've always been interested a cyclical form of story telling. In this piece James [Kirby's son]is swimming in a pool in the south of France, where many years ago, in this same location, the Romans had baths with tiled pools.

I've come up with a presentation strategy for *In Search of the Baths of Constantine*: a circular form in this linear space. On the desks in the auditorium I'm setting up small iMacs (if I can get them donated) that have flat plasma screens and DVD players. The iMacs will be scattered among the seats in the room and other seats will be open for sitting. I have cut the original timeline into different segments and made DVDs that loop. Each screen will play a looped section, starting at different parts in the timeline. No matter where you sit in the auditorium you'll have a different experience of the piece; either you will be right next to a screen and see only that one screen, or far enough away to see many screens. What excites me about this presentation is that the piece is about a movement between surfaces: the surface of the water and looking through the water to the tiles on the bottom, the surface of the pixel break up and the material quality of the digital zoom. This spatial movement is now in the space itself as the small flat panel screens are both like tiles and pixels.

T: *I feel much affinity with what you've just said, especially with this notion of dilating time, and how meaning should merge from the entirety of a gesture rather than from, let's say, a juxtaposition of cuts. One of the structural devices used in the fiction film that I'm working on now,* Night Passage, *is precisely the gesture as a story of its own — the integrity of a gesture, whether it is a visual or musical one; the gesture of the camera in its stillness and choreography for example. While existing in relation to other components, each camera gesture is independent. Each has its own beginning and ending. It's a way of acknowledging the witnessing and the autonomy of the hand that is involved — the hand as work, so that we don't even need to call it a hand . . .*

K: Gesture's a good word. Hand to eye coordination. I'm just interrupting, but in *The Unfettered Mind*, Takuan Soho's book about martial arts, the practice is to train your mind so there's no stopping. I was thinking of gesture in this way whether one is editing or looking, it's now—there's no gap between the thought and the gesture.

T: *Yes, the word 'gesture' is perhaps better because it is already a form of choreography — in my case, one that arises from the individuated time of each scene, for example. It's always a potential dance. The specificity of one move calls for that of another; once you stop, you go somewhere with it. The hand has connotations that may evoke a mysti-fying tradition of painting. Or else, it brings to mind the work, not only of people who sit in front of the computer and punch the deck, but an entire line of workers involved in every product, the codes and conventions of each process—all this is still the hand for me.*

[Working with the gesture] was one of the biggest challenges we faced in the shooting of Night Passage, *for example. Rather than having a scene that one cuts up into smaller pieces to be shot separately, and reconstructed in alternation with the master shot in the*

editing process (an approach that allows one to bypass a lot of problems, especially those of mise-en-scene and of acting), each scene was to be shot in one gesture. When you work with the integrity and autonomy of the gesture, the cutting up into smaller pieces for better consumption of a story does appear like a mere convention, and despite their efficacy, you don't want to fall prey to these facile solutions that compromise the creative approach. So perhaps this is an interesting area about which you could speak a little bit more, because I think it has also to do with this new turn in your work, which new technology seems to put to advantage.

K: True, it's not the gesture that is like dance or say that Maya Deren talked about, choreography from shot to shot and movement to movement. It's a relationship between the materials, the hand, and the technology, so that nothing is privileged. So when I shoot, it's not the image that I've shot that is sacred. That's the initial sort of experience. Then the experience of digitizing it into the computer is again another gesture. And then exporting it out to tape is another gesture. So that each interaction is a fresh response to the material.

T: *. . . that arises with the built-in layers—this constant move from one set of formation of image to another. In other words, rather than focusing only on the visual aspect of the image or on what comes immediately to the eye, you're also calling attention to the whole of the sequencing itself, to the question of duration or of body-and-machine design, or to something else happening, so that a shift of focus away from the eye-dominated image of the experimental world is effected.*

K: It's not about the image per se, it is not about the lyricism of a certain notion of experimental work. The interesting thing for me about working in the digital realm is that moving in time is so fluid. In film we can go forward, we can optically print to go backward, but the form is still linear. In film I worked hard to create the sense of cyclical time, meetings of present moments mapped onto and through larger cycles of time, both structurally in linear films and with looping the film itself. Now we can work with these gestures in time so fluidly, we can move backward and forward and loop so easily. This time sense of the gesture, this quality where objects and materials are time, is more available because it's so easy for us to see and manipulate. It's always been there and certain filmmakers have been exploiting this area in film, where the temporality is not determined by characters or drama, but the "in time-ness" of things—objects, frames, etc.—experiencing time. It's just through this technology, this way of working with time has become more available.

T: *I agree. You point very specifically to this aspect of digital technology which allows us to break away from the dominance of linear time, a time which experimental filmmakers historically worked hard at undermining. Certainly, digital technology has facilitated this task, allowing us effortless fluidity in time as you mentioned. In my case, I've always talked about time and cultural encounter in terms of double and multiple spiral movements. Rather than viewing knowledge, research, progress and meaning as a straight line with opposites at its extremes—observer and observed, insider and outsider, native and settler, home and abroad, woman and man, and so on—one can view dwelling and traveling as a single reality to be lived as a multiplicity of double spiraling movements that*

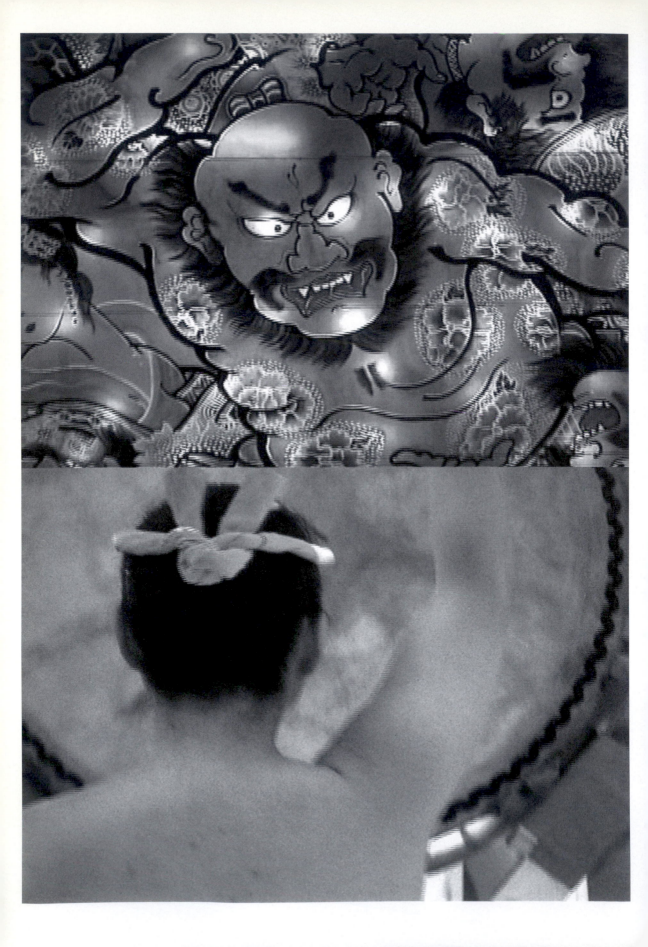

sometimes come together and other times don't. Beginnings and endings—that theatri-
cal space you were talking about—are no more than constructed temporalities. Time
becomes spatial, not only with installation work, but also with any 'text' work, whether
the latter is a book, a film, a video, a dance, or a sculpture. Ironically enough, today's
new technology can promote a sense of time that has always been available to us, but
which we've grown blind to with the pervasive rationality and linearity of modernization:
cosmic time—a time qualified by many as "timeless" because it cannot be confined to
the time of reason and of work as we know it.

K: A time that is bigger than we are. Einstein's revolution has finally happened visually for us, the relativity of time. Time/space is no longer tied to moving at 24 frames
per second or 30 frames per second, but we can actually pull it apart and collapse it on
top of itself. This moment is stacked with moments that I can't even imagine all
around the world, simultaneously available with a click. The interface too is something operating in time. We can also use these interfaces to articulate time. We have
cosmic time, in terms of how we can pull material apart, but we also have the very real
time that it actually takes for something to download into the computer. This time
reminds us of moving through actual space. We have the time that the hard disk takes
to locate digitized material. All these interfaces articulate time.

T: *But don't you think—it's just a question because I have no idea where to go with*
this—there's some kind of distinction to be made between this ultra-precise time that you
mention, and the time of programmed work and visibility that regulates our lives—more
like these little segments that we have to square ourselves with in order to function
"successfully" in society? For example, it's not a matter of confining ourselves to produc-
ing a program that can only be broadcast on mainstream television if it fits into such
dominant timeframes as: 26:40 minutes; 56:40 minutes or 86:40 minutes. Rather, it's a
matter of being able, let's say, to act minutely on the "Timeline"—which is more like
a map of the paths we finely create with time in producing sound and image. It's almost
a miracle.

K: It's incredible. Suddenly there are not the same boundaries. That's what makes
sense to me, when you say cosmic time. You can program to move through a timeline
according to other parameters. I can specify movement by saying, if there's 'x' amount
of density, move at 'x' speed. It's like getting inside the image. The image is a map to
other ways of looking and what we see on the surface is no longer determining everything. It's become very fluid between the image and time and other dimensions one
can choose to articulate. There seemed to be some kind of hierarchy with the image at
the top; now there is no gap between these events.

T: *Hearing you now reminds me of a conversation I had with viewers after a recent*
screening of The Fourth Dimension. *In this video or digital film, the train in Japan is*
featured as a main "character" together with the ritual drum. They are, in other words,
the double rhythms of modernization and tradition. It was great to see how some viewers
immediately responded to this image of the train, which I used at length in the work also
to refer to the "portable window" that video offers. The train rider and the video viewer
are linked in ritualized optical time; they occupy similar representative positions, sitting

in one place while traveling fast with light or window images. Even though we speed through Japan, as spectators we are static and immobile. The viewers mentioned further linked this with the birth of cinema—of the celluloid, or the film footage as a locomotive of projected still images, which explained the great fascination filmmakers had for the train at the time.

K: That's great because like the Lumiere Brothers, I feel that we're at that kind of moment in time too, a moment in the development of new technologies and new vocabularies.

T: *But for me there's a difference with that initial fascination with movement in mechanical time—a shot of a train arrival could then, like in later 3D-films, give the powerful impression that the train was coming straight toward the audience. Today, we seem to be drawn in by the opposite: it's no longer so much a fascination with movement, as a fascination with speed in stillness. Just sit still and everything is activated at full speed! At least, this was how I worked with the train image in* The Fourth Dimension. *A statement in the narration also mentions the computer mapping, with lights on wall panels in Tokyo, of the daily crisscrossing whereabouts of over 150 bullet trains. It's a map of time at the speed of light. The trajectories of hundreds of trains are being traced with precision on this luminous map. The notion of the "Timeline" as I discussed earlier comes back to mind here, and your description of moving inside time with speed without being subjected to the image is very relevant. What we have is an event that is very specific—controllable down to the tiniest detail—and yet an event, as you say, whose boundaries remain fluid and diffused. Again, this is something very different from the mechanical movement of the train.*

K: We share this interest with trains because of the piece *Off the Tracks*, which I made while in France. The digital camera can offer us new ways of seeing, ways that I can't see with my eyes. This is a bit similar to your mention of speed with stillness. With my little consumer camera I can see through the LCD screen what I can't see in real life. When I leave the shutter open the image is frozen a moment, yet the sound continues. The time of "actual time" is embedded in the image, but through all the movement there is a slight stillness. This is much like Sufi dancing, finding stillness through movement. Traveling through the landscape, looking out of the window, I thought a lot about the tradition of the frame in both painting and in cinema. Here framing is not only space but also time.

One of the pleasures of making work is discovery. Each step of the process is exciting. With film it is that moment for me in the car when I unwind the film I just picked up from the lab. With the video camera, it is very immediate, I can't see as I see with the camera with my own eyes, so that even catching the image is an experience that's different, than exists in another realm and is terribly exciting. Holding the camera and looking at the LCD screen instead of holding the camera to my eye has also changed the way I shoot.

Let's come back to the train. This conversation about the camera is tied to the train. My interest in moving through space at 200 miles an hour, or in France I'm thinking 200 miles an hour—I think the Japanese trains go even faster—is that you start to see the image in a way that you can't unless photographed. In *Off the Tracks* I was interested in dealing with these aspects of movement and stillness. There is a sensation of movement on every plane except the one of the lamp. The landscape is a blur that is both the speed of the train and the speed of the shutter.

I was interested in showing a stage of James' development as well, his movement from the realm of the mother to the realm of the father. When James sees that I'm zooming in to the sky, he says, 'Are we going off the tracks?' because he doesn't understand the photographic process, how the lens can move us through space. It's what I'm thinking too—especially with the digital zoom-- except I'm too sophisticated to say it out loud.

T: *So James was looking into the camera?*

K: Yes he was watching the little screen. He could see what was being photographed on the screen as it is happening, yet what he sees on the screen is different from what he sees out the window. This aspect of shooting with the shutter open is compelling to me. It allows me to see in a way that I can't see with my own eyes and gives me the landscape fresh again.

T: *I like what you said concerning the landscape that comes back to you fresh. With film, such a process has always retained its magical effect on me. Most important is the time and the waiting involved in the different stages of production—you see, you shoot, and as the developed footage comes back to you, you face the otherness inherent in every image. You may then see something new that you haven't seen before, something registered by the camera eye and now imprinted on celluloid. As you edit the film, you create anew with the intervals generated by the shifting relations between seen and filmed realities. There's no immediate gratification and each stage brings with it a different layer of creativity. In the case of digital technology it's less relevant to speak about stages since these become much more fluid—not only can you see right away how the camera sees, but what comes back to you fresh are all three or four layers of landscaping rather than one. Here, time and image are highly compressed and standardized solutions can also minimize creative intervention. Is there something specific that determines your choice of a landscape when you shoot it? Rockscape or mountainscape for example, as differentiated from the landscapes of flatland or of forest—how is that specificity translated in digital technology and how would the latter enhance the layers of freshness we are to receive?*

K: I made a stab at trying to understand this question through a piece called *Out of Step*, in which I played with the difference in the movement of the body through space and the movement of the image as it collapses in a digital space. In this case I physically walk through the landscape, through a field of grass, over rocks and down a path of red earth. The walk begins at the same point on all screens, but quickly accelerates or decelerates out of synch with the other screens as the image and the sound are transformed through each re-digitization of the image. As the movement of the image changes and is broken up by each subsequent fast forwarding, the rewind break-up of pixels reveals different spaces on top of one another. I am especially excited by this overlap of spaces. In re-digitizing, different spaces, different moments in time are

collapsed. We hover between spaces and experience "the movement of movement" even as we hear the sound of birds and walking in "real" space.

Film is a landscape medium, really, because you can step into that wonderful deep space through the screen. Hi-8 video was not a landscape medium for me; it worked better in close-up. I really like hovering between these spaces in the digital realm. Entering into the deep space of the screen and being on the surface, like the way a hummingbird moves through space.

T: *That's one of the major contributions of your work. You really make use of the video image, not only as it is presented to our eyes, but also in its formation. I am thinking here about, let's say, the rectangular form and stillness of the film image as differentiated from the video image which is constantly in formation via a scanning mechanism. We can't really have a "still" in video, and a freeze frame in this perpetual scanning is rather ironical. As a statement in* The Fourth Dimension *says, rather than talking about motion picture, one can talk about "pictures on the move." Your notion of a hovering position is wonderful. For years, since I started incorporating video in my work, I thought that the rendering of landscape was precisely the one area in which video seemed to fall way behind film. And yet, to say that is to ignore what the video image and its scanning mechanism can do. Working on that edge where one hovers anew between two landscapes or between the two- and three-dimensional can be wonderful!*

K: You do that in the *Fourth Dimension* when we move through the landscape on the train and we feel that we're hovering. It's very contemporary. We couldn't see this kind of thing unless it was made now. One couldn't actually observe that way without today's technology.

T: *To find this space for landscape imaging in video was quite important because, as I said, that was one of the areas in which I thought the medium was weakest.*

K: I know. For years I bought into the idea of the beauty of the film image, and that you could only really get a certain quality of the image with film. I held onto film for a while at great expense. Working with dollar signs buzzing was difficult. I feel very comfortable now working between media and between disciplines, but we live in a more interdisciplinary era now. It's still something that I'm actually grappling with, this loyalty to film, or this interest in the photographic process. Film is a fascinating process even if I haven't been able to put it inside a camera for several years. I am interested in working with the light sensitiveness and object-ness of film and I like to reference the history of film and be in conversation with filmmakers across time. I remember once you were talking about some footage in *Naked Spaces* and how it wound up with a particular color. The film had aged or was light-struck or something happened while you were traveling around with it that made it an incredible red. This element of fragility and temperature seems important to me.

T: *But more important is the fact that this strong awareness of the photographic process is not all there is to your work—even when you were using film, which can be so eloquent on the photographic process. I'm not talking about the significance of content here; it's something else, and it links up with your interest in installation. Let's take, for example, the point you raised about surface and depth in relation to spectatorship. The opposition set up between these two forms of space—surface and depth—remains well encoded in the art world, that is, in the world of Western metaphysics. (Jean-Luc) Godard's films are eloquent examples of rupture with such a divisional view. He didn't need to go into all this psychological depth à la Bergman in order to portray depth, he radically dwelled on the surface, on the two-dimensional reality of the film image to deal with the social complexities of our time. Surface is not equated with superficiality, and depth is not equated with truth. There's no hierarchy involved when depth, like surface, is just another dimension. Working intensely with the material limit of a surface can open up an infinitely new sense of depth.*

I'm thinking here of the many projects you have done that play with these dimensions, like Outside the Gold Frame, *where you have the film projected beyond the frame and then you have the film projected inside the frame. Also, the piece on the ocean, the C to C project, whose experience was truly powerful when I first saw it. Not only was I carried away by the sensuality of the image—that expanding movement of the sea/C—and by the specific acknowledgement of the photographic process in the installation lay out, I was also struck by the fragmentation . . . —almost like a pulverization of the image—in space. The piece has a simultaneous foreground and background; you were working with the two planes at once.*

K: I love hearing you talk about my work! You're so generous because you understand my concerns. I really do want to talk about these tensions, not in a dualistic way, but as pressures between filmic dimensions. After you work for a certain amount of time you start to understand certain dialogues, certain conversations that you have with yourself. Not only the idea of circular time, but this circle of surface, depth, inside, outside, so that the "landscape" and the "inside" are not that separate. There are themes that I've been coming back to over and over again. One can look at the work and say, 'oh that's landscape' because in art we've conveniently divided things into landscapes and portraits, but they're part of a cycle of investigation about human states of being and philosophies and feelings. So that a piece that's about the ocean really is about a heartbeat, or a piece about my son is about the landscape.

T: *In relation to this tradition of portraits and landscape, it's interesting to see how video, like film, can be very strong in portraits, partly because its eloquence lies in the close-up shot. But to deal with landscape in video, we need to step out of the trap in which we get caught when we hold onto a certain idea of the beautiful—of the kind of deep space film is able to convey, for example.*

K: That was very liberating for both of us; to jettison that particular notion of deep space. The other thing that has happened, that makes working different now, is that video comes with sync sound. We spent many years, both of us, with non sync sound cameras. The sound was a total construction next to the image. There was a space that one created between the image and the sound, which for me was very exciting. And then, when I discovered video and digital video, using a consumer camera, the sound and the image are linked, they come together. I've wanted to give them that integrity. When I began working in HI-8 I was interested to find that the camera itself

would make sounds, the zoom lens made a wonderful squeaking sound. Some viewers thought I overused that sound of the zoom. I was fascinated by it, partly because at that point I was working a lot with a musician, Glenn Spearman. We performed together and the zoom became a part of my instrument the camera, like the keys on Glenn's saxophone.

There is not only the fluidity of the image that we're talking about, but we have that state in the sound, too. So that the notion of the soundtrack and how one constructs the sound is also a whole other area of exploration that I feel that I'm only beginning to scratch. I was very influenced by (Jean-Marie) Straub and (Danièle) Huillet, how their sync-soundness was so profound. I never thought of "sync-sound" as a rule to stick by for myself because, as in film, I was interested in the space between the image and the sound. Now I'm compelled by the sync-ness of video. As I digitize into the computer I can hear the speed of the tape, when I scrub in the time line I can hear the gaps between moments in time. I can see what's happening and I can hear it also. Sound has a form of abstraction that's very different from the image. With image we're seeing something that we can name, so to speak, but as we jump around in the time-line in sound, it's something else. It's very musical.

T: *You're right as far as recording sound with consumer cameras is concerned. In* The Fourth Dimension, *since I was dealing with aspects of the culture that link it to new technology's promotion of speed, portability, and mobility, it was ideal to shoot with this little consumer's camera that one could just put in one's pocket or innocuously display in most circumstances without making people feel uncomfortable. There's no need to spend time on elaborate set up; since shooting with such a tool is quick and effortless, you are always "strolling" with images. Such a mobility can be seen in the very image produced, for the camera and body movement generated by a camera you hold in your hand is very different from the one generated by a camera positioned on your shoulder. The same applies to the painless but noisy recording of sound with a microphone built in the camera. Your incorporation of the very sound of the zoom may make all the difference.*

However, in the shooting of my last film, Night Passage, *the issues and aesthetics that arose were different. I did not want to have the buzzing camera sound in my sound track, so we recorded all synchronized sound separately, as with film. But, as you can imagine, the task of putting it back in sync with the image afterwards was enormous. The process was worse than with film, partly because new technology has focused its effort far more on the visual than on the audio in video production, and far more also on the recording of the image than on its editing. In response to what you said very nicely, one can affirm that perhaps because of its fluidity, it's more "natural" in video to work with built-in sync sound from the start. When you decide to record it separately, you will have to deal with some unexpected difficulties, since synchronization in the editing and outputting processes of video on the computer can at times be quite frustrating. So we agree, sound is a whole area to be explored in digital technology. You work at length with sound in* Altamont Pass, *or even in the piece,* C to C. *I'm tempted to ask you to come back to this last piece because somehow it seems to me to be connected to the unique nature of installation. These are the kind of works that appeal to you more than a straight film. The idea of an installation involves working with space, or with sound and image in space as event.*

K: In *C to C: Several Centuries After the Double Slit Experiment*, I was interested in the plastic space of the actual installation site and the space and time of history, both in film and in science. I wanted to work with a western tradition of landscape organization of space into a foreground, middle ground and background, and also be able to flatten these distinctions between planes. I set up frames—flags of different dimensions, on C stands. These flags, usually used for blocking or filtering light in production, by changing to satin, I used here to reflect the light. I photographed the sea. The projected waves breaking onto the flags, appear to shift from foreground, to middle ground, to background and to the far background—the deepest space being the actual space of the screen in the theatre that was closed off to be just a vertical slit. This was an allusion to Thomas Young's double slit experiment which demonstrated the wave-like interference phenomenon of light. I turned the camera off periodically while shooting and then back on so that the movement of the waves would jump and the space between the waves is clear as the film is fogged. When the camera stops and the image goes clear for the few seconds of fogged film, the entire installation space is illuminated and flattened. When the film goes clear you see the sandbags holding up the C stands.

I wanted the viewer to be aware of the filmic construction of space and that apparatus of a set and film production. It's called *C to C* as a kind of pun, because it's an image of the sea, and alludes to the lyric "Sea to Shining Sea" since I filmed at the Pacific Ocean, the end of the continental United States. Where is the construction of space, filmically? It's about these ideas of landscape, but always about the filmmaking. It also alludes to the history of film. Michael Snow's *Wavelength* winds up on a postcard of the sea, where this work starts. I play his film in the booth along with mine so if you turn around you can see his film and you hear his soundtrack. . . .

T: . . . *Why the heartbeat?*

K: It has to do with the rhythm of the ocean. The ocean is tied to the cycle of the moon, it's life.

T: *Yes. I would add here: is the ocean outside or inside? The heartbeat, which can be such a stereotypical sound in film, has regained its expansive function in the piece. It immediately brings you into your body and out, for the ocean is not merely external.*

K: Precisely. I'd like to go back a bit to continue on the subject of time. I remember a discussion after seeing *The Fourth Dimension*. You talked so beautifully about the kind of time that you wanted to explore, not only time when you travel someplace, which is also the movement through the landscape, but travel in time, through your material, that affords a kind of understanding in a culture. Could you talk a bit about this. It is one of the things I am struck by in your recent piece, and in all your work, the generosity that you have when you go somewhere. I've appreciated that you always find a fresh way of looking.

T: *You are referring here to the conversation I had with the audience when* The Fourth Dimension *was first shown in Berkeley. I think I was then discussing time in relation to the question of ritual in the work—a rather hazardous terrain to walk on, but one does* *take a risk when one works with terms too familiar to the ear and eye. Rituals are usually identified with tradition, and tradition is always equated with the old or the past. In other words, they are associated with the movement of continuity in dwelling. However, the conservative and constraining aspect of rituals—which is the more evident aspect of Japanese culture in its daily conventions and coded excesses—is only one dimension of the reality. I myself have been very critical toward certain practices in cultural anthropology focused on rituals, mainly because of the way information is retrieved, accumulated, and categorized to validate a certain "expertise" in the field. It is through such "anthropological" practices that rituals become dead practices—past, repetitive, museum-like—to our eyes. As it is well known, the retrieval and representation of tradition goes hand in hand with the invention of tradition.*

But to say this is also to say that such a circular praxis is not necessary. The scope of a ritual can be very vast. In its more inclusive sense, ritual practices involve not only the regularity in the structure of everyday life, but also the dynamic agents in the ongoing process of creating a symbolic world of meaning and truth. We are all engaged in rituals in our daily activities, and by remaining unaware of their ritual propensity, we remain in conformity. Rather than giving ourselves agency in our everyday acts, we tend to carry them out passively. I've sometimes defined artists and activists as "pathmakers," and "art," as a way of marking moments in our lives. For me, the power of Butoh dancers, for example, lies in their strong awareness of the ritual in life and death; it is actualized in their ability to transform while they perform. Similarly, one can say that media practice, at its best, is ritual performance. A work that remains alive is a work always in performance. The way technology uses us while we use them, the way we frame while being framed are interactive processes. One should treat rituals as rituals if one is to step out of the servile one-dimensional mind and turn an instrument into a creative tool.

You talked about landscapes coming to us fresh thanks to the photographic process; ritual can be said here to lie not only over there (in the subject filmed or in the culture observed), but over here with the camera and myself. It is the ritualized encounter between subjectivities, between human and machine, between virtual and real, between ear, eye, and the other senses that determines the uniqueness of the work or the performance. One has to learn the rituals of new technology if one is to make reality speak anew and differently to the viewer. Placed in this inclusive context, rituals can offer a field of relations in which new, challenging interactions between past and present are possible. The fourth dimension of cinema, which is the dimension of time, is materialized on screen thanks to the attention brought to the diverse rituals that give the video its form(s)—and content. The many times involved in the layering of the work are here all put to play: musical, historical, sociopolitical time, as well as montage time, optical time; the time of festivities, of traveling, of witnessing, and of viewing; the time, so to speak, of both electronic and spiritual light.

I have further linked the question of ritual to that of boundary. The stifling timeframes and boundaries we come up with in our lives for control purposes are innumerable. We spoke earlier about the time of rationality and reason, the normalized time of work defined in terms of packaged goods and services, the time of marketing, exhibiting, and of compulsory consumption. But whether boundaries confine or enhance depend on how one conceives them: they are markers of both endings and beginnings. Some can only

close down; others close only to open out further. I'll focus here on viewing time for exam-
ple. By that, I mean both the makers as time markers—mediamakers are the first viewers
of their work (that's the time when they conceive images, capture via the camera and edit
the shots, for example)—and the viewers as time feelers—the way the spectators remain
consumers or become participants in their reception of the work. Let's take the case of my
film Naked Spaces, *which is two hours and fifteen minutes long. The experience of this*
film's time has been very extreme among viewers: some were restless, finding it excruciat-
ingly long (even though they have no problem sitting through commercial narratives
over two hours long); others could hardly come up with words to share the intense ecstatic
state into which they were taken. The latter didn't seem to have enough of the film; one
even told me that the film should have a theater all to itself because it should be screened
continuously everyday. (Interestingly, new technology does contribute to partly fulfill such
a wish, for this is how Naked Spaces *is being screened at* Documenta 11 *in Germany—*
seventeen years after the statement was made, albeit with DVD projection.)

Time is plastic. It is what we are. Not only does it differ according to people's diverse
sensitivities, it also differs according to the mood and the context in which the same
person happens to be: a friend of mine, for example, who was transported by her first
viewing of Naked Spaces *and invited me to show it at her institution, told me (somewhat*
irritated) during the second viewing with her impatient audience, that I should definitely
cut down the length of the film. Time seems to shrink or to expand according to the
degree of one's availability. One can say that disaster times, such as the events of
September 11 in the US or the events lived by people in war situations around the world,
have the power to wipe away everything that one narrowly holds on to—the small mea-
surements devised to keep one's life on tracks. People who have come out of disaster often
speak of "waking up" from sleepwalking and the first thing they realize is that time
cannot be bought. The time many of us profoundly value proves here not to be the
money-time of success and failure, but the time of friendship and of intimate relation-
ship, which we tend to take for granted in hectic modern life. It is as if, with all this
promotion for faster-always-faster and more-always-more in new technology, it takes the
disruption of a catastrophe or a disaster to really show us the importance of slowing
down.

K: I have often been interested in what happens during a calamity. The time of crisis
or time of disaster is a special form of time. Time opens up when we're out in the street
in our bathrobes or just before we crash in a car accident. I worked with this kind
of time in both *Across the Street,* and *Sharon and the Birds on the Way to the Wedding.*
I agree that this kind of disaster time makes us more human, more aware of our neigh-
bors. It tests us also. Social codes break down and we act differently. Which is what we
have seen so much of during and after the events of September 11th.

Related to this kind of in-between time is the liminal time of transformation. I work
with this time in *Sharon and the Birds,* between the state of being single and the state
of being married and in *Off the Tracks,* the movement from the realm of the mother to
the realm of the father. These are spaces outside of coded rituals, not like the wedding
ceremony itself that has a form, but important marking points in life that don't necessarily have containers, so the transitions can be difficult or confusing. This confusion
has been a fertile place for me to explore. . . .

We can use new technology to mark time and use the tools to articulate change, I don't think the tools have to use us. A couple of things that you said really interest me and I feel very close to. This idea you mentioned of the different kinds of times that one can experience. That pulse can come from different places, depending on the project. I've often felt with my work that I've been trying to articulate another kind of time, another kind of pace that's not about a narrative pace, but of circular time or ritualized time or the quiet time that is in-between activities. Each of us is in touch with biological time differently, cultural time differently, even the linear time of a particular story we're in touch with differently. I've become interested in finding ways of working with multiple screens with loops of different lengths, so that pieces will unfold depending on the viewer's time commitment with the piece. If viewers want to spend three seconds, they will get one thing; if viewers wants to spend an hour they will get something else. This is what happens in life. Relationships shift.

T: *This leads us back to the idea you raised earlier, that despite the overwhelming tendency to consume passively, it is new technology that allows us to enter these different layers of time creatively. The example you gave of working with a different time-pulse and time-shift is precisely what we are invited to do with new media.*

K: I'm beginning see that I have to understand not only the interfaces that we purchase, but to understand the software enough to manipulate it or even to write my own software. As artists we need to understand the tools enough to be able to really work with them, as we did in film. I want to understand how to navigate inside the computer. It's not just the flatbed equivalent of the editing machine, it's a whole other kind of language that is now available. It's such an exciting opportunity because in a way it's closer to how I've always seen, without knowing that that was the case. Do you know what I mean?

T: *Yes. I have similar feelings because when you talk about timing in the lab, you actually hit on the issue of production relations which new technology can help to shift. In film, the question of color timing, for example, remains a realm of the lab specialist (who may also be an artist in his own right). Whereas with digital video, color correction tools are not only included in accessible editing programs like Final Cut Pro, they also allow one to intervene more minutely in the formation process of the image, rather than to proceed from cut to cut or from shot to shot as in film (as mainstream filmmakers like to remind us, the shot is the golden basic unit of film).*

K: Before the shot was the building block, and you put all your shots together and you built your architecture over time. Now your architecture is built within a gesture that is larger than a discreet shot. The architecture can be constructed with an infinite number of gestures, density, color intensity or any other parameter you choose to come up with.

T: *I would like to come back to the notion of installation, since this is the direction you have taken in your more recent works. How do you see the current situation with installation works—the space of exhibition, the kind of work that's being exhibited, and the way "installation" has grown with the advent of digital video, for example?*

K: Some artists got frustrated with the small number of viewers who would come into the "experimental cinema" space. There was an interesting conversation in galleries that happened up until maybe the mid '70s, and then in our generation conversations between the plastic arts and the film arts seemed quite separate. Museums would have a cinema, but there wouldn't often be cinema within the galleries of the museum. In the last few years with the advent of digital technology there has been an explosion of media installation in both galleries and museums.

I've become more and more interested in working with the object-ness of film, but not necessarily in the sense of it as a product, an original art object.

T: *. . . With the film viewing apparatus, there's a number of dividing lines between what's in and what's out; what's seen and what's not. While we look at the screen in front of us, the projection booth and camera are behind us. Whereas in the installation space, we can bring in the booth and the projector, and have diverse elements materially present. We can move inside and interact with the imaging process.*

K: I love working with this aspect of the projection space. But actually, I don't see much of that happening. I see a kind of invisible projection in a lot of installations. They could be films or videos in a theatrical space. Although there were great examples at the "Into the Light show" at the Whitney, did you see that? A lot of those artists really thought about the space of projection. But there seems to be a gap from that powerful work of the 60's and 70's and now. There are a few wonderful artists who have been working spatially, but in much of what I see that whole articulation of the space is missing.

T: *We dealt with this issue at length when we were working on our installation,* Nothing But Ways. *The only reason for having an installation in that huge space at The Yerba Buena Center for the Arts (San Francisco, 1999), was to make use of it. It was in exploring the space we had and putting it to maximum play, that we came up with this very large-scale and yet minimal installation. This is not quite the same as having an outdoor, site-specific project. For me, most installation works lay emphasis on the object exhibited rather than on the space or on the frame. What attracts museums are object-oriented pieces that can be conveniently transported from one space to another. Instead of engaging as container-contained process (rather than as message or artifact), most of the time, just like with film where people tend to see only the content or the form of the work, the focus is on the objects on display and the single idea these often convey. One recognizes the same problem across media, despite the claim, with installations, to encompass multiple viewpoints—an attempt to break away from the frontal film screen.*

K: One of the reasons I loved and still do love making film and video work, is that there is no object—it can't be consumed in that way. It is an experience. This is the problematic relationship to the gallery space—if you don't have an object, how can you have a market around it? So you have to be able to market it and therefore the space is not something that you can market. It is exciting to have the projection in space—it's a totally different experience when film is in a space, and you can move around it and the body can move through the space, casting shadows.

T: *I found the piece you hint at earlier, Anthony McCall's* Line Describing a Cone, *to be extremely exciting. The piece brings into focus the whole apparatus of film projecting and viewing, while offering itself as a hybrid between film, performance, graphic design and sculpture. The problem with object-oriented pieces is precisely the absence of such boundary crossing—one that deals with the very potentials of "installation." The claim to multiplicity, decentralization, interactivity, and temporality in viewing still consti-tutes the core of arguments that champion installations in the gallery space. And yet, one hardly sees any major challenge of the viewing subject or any structural shift of per-ception in these works when the focus remains centralized on the one idea materialized by the object displayed (even if this object is a transmitting device), when multiplicity and interactivity of views remain a question of variations around a main theme. There has been a time when the art object was displayed to defy its own status as art object, to resist what could be consumed and marketed as "art"—in short, to ridicule the whole system that supported the art world. But that kind of conversation has greatly dwindled, and the more conveniently packaged the object of installation is today, the better it cir-culates in gallery and museum venues.*

K: Right, it's easier to float it from space to space, but it's not exploring the space sculpturally. If one is going to take it off the proscenium screen and into a space, how is that space being used? Why have it in space? Otherwise have it on the screen. The project has another set of questions when one makes the work site specific or site dependent.

T: *On the one hand, the less space-specific the object for display, the more mobile it is. On the other hand, rather than rethinking the activity of installing, and conceiving the work as a different way of creating in relation to, or as a way of drawing new relation-ships in space, for example, installation often turns out to be the mere execution of an idea. So the idea becomes marketable because you can bring it anywhere and just repeat that idea. It's not really linked to . . .*

K: . . . its spatial qualities. I do want to go back to this idea of film as an object. I think I came to this idea of "an object" as I realized that some film or digital work could exist as an object, but that this object-ness was a different thing than installation work.

T: *It seems adequate to link your notion of "film as an object" to that of "translation," in its more inclusive sense. Film as film calls attention to both the means of translation and the impossibility of translation, which is the paradoxical reality involved in image making. Most people think of film in terms of photo realism—as captured real world— so when one uses film as film, when the reality of film and its apparatus or the process of creating sound images and meanings constitutes the very subject of the work, one's work becomes incomprehensible to many people's eyes. Film and translation as a reality on their own tend to remain invisible or non-recognizable in their materialization. Paradox-ically, films are considered most abstract when they deal with the very concrete materiality of film. In today's technology where the person's presence and physical existence is on the line, perhaps one can say that virtual reality is at its most concrete when it deals with its own abstract-ness, its own virtuality. To learn how to navigate the system creatively, "real" and "virtual" constantly need to return to us fresh.*

K: Yes, "translation" film as film, not film as image. There is a difference in work that deconstructs the interface of projection, production and distribution and work that is on a single screen and functions in a gallery space or screening space in a conversation with the history of cinema/ painting. I have been moving between these practices. Concurrent to the Cinematheque screenings I will be showing some of the recent digital work at Ampersand International Arts. Most of the work will be shown on plasma screens mounted on the wall, similar to the way I showed *Photons in Paris: image encoding.3* at the Whitney. At Ampersand all five pieces in the series will be shown on small screens mounted on the wall. The screens themselves are connected very visibly to small DVD players. The work is situated between a moving cinematic painting and sculptural relief. This work is not intended to be projected and is not intended as installation. I wanted to work with the kind of light that comes out of the plasma screen rather than from a projection. When the light is embedded inside the screen, in the form of squares, like pixels, then it mirrors the pixel infrastructure of the work.

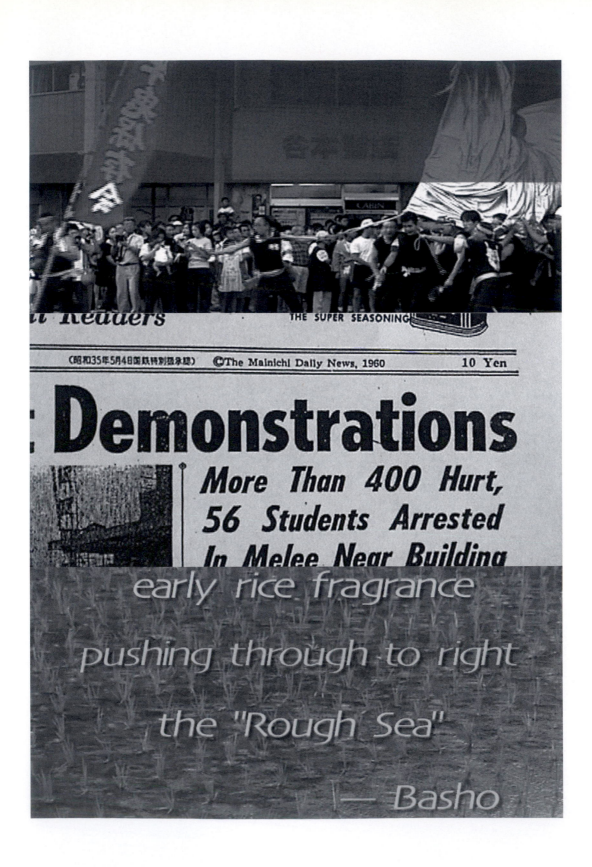

THE SUPER SEASONING

(昭和35年5月4日国鉄特別扱承認) ©The Mainichi Daily News, 1960   10 Yen

Demonstrations

**More Than 400 Hurt,
56 Students Arrested
In Melee Near Building**

early rice fragrance

pushing through to right

the "Rough Sea"

— Basho

FILMSCRIPT

Japan, 2001. 86:40 mins, digital, color
Produced by Jean-Paul Bourdier and Trinh T. Minh-ha
Photographed, written and edited by Trinh T. Minh-ha
Music by The Construction of Ruins with
Greg Goodman, (un) prepared piano and *objets d'intérieur*
and by Shoko Hikage, Koto, Bass Koto and vocals
Distributed by Women Make Movies Inc., New York;
The British Film Institute, London (UK);
Freunde der Deutschen Kinemathek, Berlin (Germany);
and DnC Media (Korea).

JIKANDES— IT'S TIME

tell me, is it the fog or is it me?

show a country, speak of a culture, in whatever way,
and you'll enter into fiction while yearning for invisibility

ravers' madness
a new form of kindness

how tall is Japan?
height, weight, age?

(on screen)

AGE

PASS

OF

RITES

RITES OF PASSAGE

Japanese written on every facets of life
calligraphied in the thousand plays of neon signs

                              the speed of light

where are you now?
          in a train
          facing the window-screen
          second-class seat
          speeding through Japan's likeness

                                        Kogo tokitsukusazare
          As people say here, "in a good talk, don't explain everything"

                                        GISHIKI

Rituals
                    and the formation of identity
the skill of behavior, the craft of framing time, the art of paths

     why travel, I would say, if not to be in touch with the ordinary in
     non-ordinary ways; to feel and think ordinarily while experiencing
     what can later become the extra-ordinary in an ordinary frame

                                        SHINKANSEN

the bullet train
part of a new class structure
the luxury of going faster
while sitting in one place

               start in a room sealed with darkness
and a door or a window immediately etches itself onto the viewer's
mind

again, it's that unbearable fellow
traveler who won't stay behind,
whom one cannot get rid of

opening at dawn, closing at dusk

sorrows forming and falling away
heavy
like drops of water from a lotus leaf

every day from a blossoming lotus
something's emerging
every day from deep in the mud
someone's being reborn

SUKURIN RIZUMU — (on screen) SCREEN RHYTHM

painting, photography and cinema used to offer different realms of
images
today the gap becomes the bridge,
what tends to separate film from video can offer a passage
a world, not of motion pictures, but of images on the move

pushing, no piercing
the match lasts the times it takes
for horns to unlock
no crisis, no bloodshed
when "gravity is the root of lightness" (Tao te-ching)

the seated interface carries with it a danger
both geophysical and spiritual:
that of body losing touch with body

everyday, controlled by a computer brain in Tokyo
over 150 bullet trains crisscross Japan
their whereabouts neatly mapped in tiny lights on wall panels

the truly real world is there where you see trains. For Soseki Natsume,
nothing represents better the civilization of the 20th century than the
train. Hundreds of people crammed in a box that rumbles along
heartlessly. All taken at uniform speed to the same station. . . . He
wrote: "Modern civilization uses every possible means to develop
individuality, and having done so, tries everything in its power to
stamp it out. It allots a few square yards to each person, and tells him
that he is free to lead his life as he pleases within that area. At the
same time it erects railings around him, and threatens him with all
sorts of dire consequences if he should dare to take but one step
beyond their compass. . . . The railway train which blunders ahead
blindly into the pitch of darkness is one example of the very obvious
dangers which abound in modern civilization."

inside outside, host guest
the role assigned like the role assumed
at first seems fixed
carefully enforced, scrupulously performed
but once the initiation rites have passed
from one closure to another
the inside surreptitiously draws its elements from outside
without being any less inside
meticulously adapted, extended, and transformed

nothing is natural,
for the natural in its most natural is carefully created

(heard in Japanese, read in English)
Kono waro ga kochira muku made suwari miyo
katte kakusanu ono ga memboku —*Ko doja*
(on screen) *"Look at how long this fellow has been sitting here;*
our original face has never been hidden" —*Ko doja*

in the matted room
a solitary painting
barely line, barely shape
that frail shadow
of a boddhisatva
shading its human frame

the mask:
what makes a face into a molding of society and history

performing one's gender is part of the boring social contract
commenting on the sexual ambivalence in girls comic books,
Imaizumi Fumiko insists that girls' "deepest desire is to be neither
male nor female"—they take on a sexless role that departs from the
adult women's subservient role in life, feeling that reality and dreams
can be reversed by changing male and female appearances.

only when behavior carefully rehearsed becomes collective
do differences fully take on their individual color

the relentless pressures to conform
the endless demand for freedom

GISHIKI

like nature, human nature itself is carefully molded

GISHIKI

the choreography of everyday activities
and of every stage role
has been kept alive for centuries

GISHIKI

suddenly here I am

carried by the cadence and the swift metamophoses of the line
its continuity, tensions, improvisations and repetitions

the exact train system mirrors the structure of the society it serves
machines and people work in mutual accord
once the choice for a destination is made
it can be altered any time in any way during the journey
for the fare registered by the machine
can always be readjusted by the human hand

(On screen) **HUMAN TIME — MACHINE TIME**

itineraries are modified as so desired
without any fuss or distrust
for no one seeks to beat the system
when treated with mutual respect
human and machine share the same devotion to duty

the infinite lines of railways regulating the urban space

On the Noh dance, Okakura Kakuzo decreed: "the standard of excellence is an infinite suggestiveness, naturalism the one thing to be condemned."

Nothing is more lustrous than ice
—Hitori Goto

Time
—time frozen in its movement.

long ago Dogen warned:
"If you neglect the formality of guest and host,
you can understand neither the true nor the phenomenal"

In the seventh century during his visit of the Shadow's Cave in the kingdom of Nagara hara, the Chinese traveling monk Xuan Zang noted that, in olden times, one could see there the shadow of Buddha, as radiant as his natural appearance, and one would have thought it was the living Buddha himself. But for the last few centuries, one has no longer seen this shadow clearly. Whatever one sees is only a weak and doubtful resemblance."

to survive,
spirituality would have to come to us from all the ordinary images of life

Kono waro ga kochira muku made suwari miyo
katte kakusanu ono ga memboku
—Ko doja

It is said that
                              when Shakyamuni lost his ordinary sight
                   one branch of a plum tree blossomed in the snow

"the principle underlying [Japanese] cultural forms," says
Nyozekan Hasegawa, "is the control of feeling"
a control ideally meant to intensify emotion without
flooding the recipient

                                        bridge, train, passenger
                                             what's in motion?

windows closed
muted soundtrack
no body movement
only the erotic rocking
of human against machine

                              landscape, image, wagon, viewer
                        what's moving in the midst of stillness?

traveling anew
with video images
put on line
displayed on screen

                                   from one spectacle to the next
                                       mobility of human sets
                                  procession of window images
                                         the landscape wired
                                            now glimpsed
                                        now no longer seen
                                         morphing changing
                                   from one minute to the next

shooting in rural Japan
one often shoots in corporate mentality
collective highlights, collective shots, collective climax
collective photography

a night heron (go-isagi)
sitting tense on one leg
ready to strike
in clear water
with one single swoop

passing through the *torii* gate,
one encounters an inside-Japan
only to be made more aware of an outside-Japan

torii gate
setting off the mundane from the spiritual

what we see passes away
the more evident becomes the background
while the minor details
go on shifting what is seen and heard

the other dimension: gaseous and liquid
because what appears evident to the eye is the straight line
normal perception is solid, geometric, clear-cut and divisive

Jikishi   jinshin
kensho   jobutsu
Sarajuge 83 sai rono
Hakuin so megane nashi hi haku

(on screen)
"direct pointing   to the human heart
seeing one's nature   becoming Buddha.
Written by the 83-year-old priest Hakuin
sitting beneath the Sala tree without his glasses"

                              "vast emptiness, nothing holy"

ingrained in modern social interaction and political performance
ritual is not compatible with industrial speed
to perform a ritual one must slow down

WOMEN'S TIME — JAPAN'S TIME

Japanese women of old are said to have this impassive look of the
mask and to live like masks, with their deepest energies turned inward
                              (according to Enchi Fumiko)

                    surface is surface
                        and yet,
              boundless is the depth of the surface
                 that neither conceals nor reveals

what if, in this journey, like Enchi and Soseki, I were to regard events
as parts of a Noh play and the people as its actors? Curbing my
emotions to get near to the Noh atmosphere; no, not to probe the
whys and wherefores of the characters' behavior and to pry into their
daily worries, but to let them move about and come to me in full lines
from a two-dimensional picture

video: a delight
for the drowsy body
the seated interface
screen against screen
mutually accessed
mutually processed
activated and shut off

trains, processions, parades,
time organized in sequences

the time of light

the San-mon gate of Nanzen-ji
massive, unique
one among the thousand gates

gates, bridges, corridors
intricate passages in time
sequences of infinity

in the Nihonshoki, the introduction of the art of gardens is linked to the arrival in the year 612 of a Korean refugee who, in order to gain residence in Japan, called attention to his talent for representation and was put in charge of tracing the figures of mount Sumeru and the bridge of Wu in the southern garden of the palace. People called him then the "pathmaker" *(michiko no takumi)*

MIENU HANA

(on screen)   not seen flower

FUKASHINA HANA

unseen flower

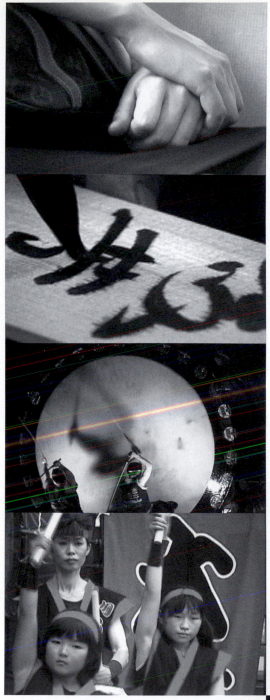

un seen FloWer

walking with Basho
the lines of a haiku come to visibility

> *"traveler's heart*
> *never settled long in one place*
> *like a portable fire"*

small, restrained, evocative—an esthetic in tune with the fragility and
uncertainty of life
a model of understatement with its shades of gray

Japan, "the home of the module unit, the first of the prefab lands"
—wrote a foreign resident (Donald Richie)

a governing system
whose organization is largely based on microstructures
and prefabricated cells

stop by the side of a merrymaking event
and a procession reveals to the mind's eye, clear and loud
as an cluster of melodic, rhythmic, action-propelling and structure-
bearing cells

the mobile people
telepresent
in a transmitted scene

where?
where to?
groping one's way
in the midst of Time
as the fog slowly dissipates
leading to a clearing
a new place, a new picture

all lie uncomfortably between
fact and fancy
there where
in the heart of an insular culture
even the mobile world
of invisible narrators
of uneven times and odd rhythms
finds its place
in the precise framing of daily activities

Zen picture: demythologized.
Open distance - nothing sacred

(heard in Japanese, then in English)
Sembutsu jochu
Sembutsu ni kiraware
Gumma tairi
Gumma ni nikumaru
Konji mokusho no jato o kujiki
Kindai dammu no kasso o minagoroshi ni su.
    Shahan shuaku no hakattoku
    Shujo shu o sou mata isso

"in the realm of the thousand Buddhas
he is hated by the thousand Buddhas
among the crowd of demons
he is detested by the crowd of demons
he crushes the silent-illumination heretics of today,
and massacres the heterodox blind monks of this
generation.
This filthy blind old shavepate
adds more foulness still to foulness" —Hakuin Zenji

May 19. Democracy was crushed by state power. The parliament forcibly adopted the revised Treaty binding Japan to the American security system.

June 16, 1960
the Asahi Evening News and the Mainichi Daily News reported the death of Kamba Michiko during a bloody demonstration against the Government of Prime Minister Kishi and the signing of the renewed Japan-US Security Treaty. Kamba Michiko, a student of Tokyo University and a well-known leader of the 20,000 Zengakuren students who besieged the legislative building, had previously been arrested for taking part in the earlier demonstration at Haneda to prevent the prime minister from leaving for the United States. The official narratives unanimously condemned the violence of the event that shook and shocked the nation, while alternative voices blamed the ultranationalists for having set the demonstrators afire by attacking them ferociously. Such an insurrection—also referred to as "bloody left-wing riots in Japan"—happening before President Eisenhower's scheduled arrival in Tokyo was said to have appalled Washington and America's President who declared "he would not permit unpleasant incidents . . . to interfere with the goodwill tour he was undertaking to improve the climate of international understanding."

Upon looking at how time is expressed in writing and how a death can express the passing of a historical age and its people, Kenzaburo Oe particularly recalls the death of Tsuburaya Kokichi, a young runner in the Olympics, who committed suicide in 1968 because, in his own words, the man was "too tired to run" for national prestige.
But, in the history of women's resistance and of women pathmakers of the sixties, it is the name of Kamba Michiko that comes to many women's lips as I inquire about the one political figure that strikes their memory.
Kamba Michiko's death may be said to have marked the turning point for the image the world had of Japan. With the repression of a civic society, what was then launched was a new image of Japan as a corporate society for which the only way to progress was the Western way.

Highly advanced and yet not independent

a global economic power struggling today to re-orient itself
to turn toward Asia without turning its back on the West

"Ambivalent Japan": isolated from other Asian nations and confined
to Her half-scrutable strangeness by the West. In America, the very
nation with which She signed the Security Treaty, suspicion is always
lurking at the slightest sign of trade competition

FUTSU

the ordinary

IJO

the extra-ordinary

part-time women's labor, the million-yen wall
full-time family shadow work
the issue of homemaking
indispensable but invisible

Japan's stigma: the lot of its millions of outcasts and others—natives,
exiled and immigrants discriminated against (the Ainu, the
Okinawan, the Burakumin, the ethnic Koreans and also the Chinese,
the workers from Southeast Asia and the Middle East)—all essential
to Japan's progress and identity as a modern nation, but confined to
the underpaid, underprivileged margins

sliding open the blinding screens
I find myself stepping suddenly into the fourth dimension

speeding: everywhere one turns, someone is trying to sell speed
the fast species

the peculiar vibrations of graphic space, graphic time
the whole of visual environment finds its dynamism in the graphic
line

keep to the time as required by tele-vision
screen space, say TV programmers
is always, always limited

but, as novelist Hisashi Inoue once said,
I don't like bonsaiism ... it's perfectly all right for some trees to grow
big and wild"

the journey unfolds through the unseen but dominant framing
of time

three times in one
present past future

as soon as one is in time
time no longer flees
standing still, it opens out

TRAIN TIME — NOH TIME
NO
NO TRAIN

Noh performance, as Soseki affirmed, is "three-tenths real emotion,
seven-tenths technique" layers upon layers, clad with "art" to weave a
tapestry of gestures of serenity that is to be found nowhere else in this
world
yet, for Enchi Fumiko, we are Noh actors moving in the screen space
of ritual, ethical life

the skill of behavior,
the craft of framing time, the art of paths
what else but the shape of living caught in the unfolding course of a
digital play?

The determination to never wage a war again, as Kenzaburo Oe remarks, is a resolve adopted not by innocent people but people stained by their own history of territorial invasion

video time: a temporal trap
remote control and the law of least action
individual inertia as the result of ever-increased speed
of programmed agency

from inside the train
looking up
at the wired sky
moving on
wireless, rootless, unplugged

Kisho Kurosawa spoke of Japanese esthetics as being primarily two-dimensional and gray. He laid focus on temporal intervals, intermediary zones and silent spaces; on the necessity to create with the *ma* of things and events, for a person without *ma* is scorned as a stupid fellow, one who lacks calm and is unable to tune in with the gray zone of Japanese culture

images have come upstream towards the traveler
they appear on the screen with each step
front foot back foot
one moves with them
one stops by the road to chat with them
and they know how to show certain things
but cannot always tell why they show things the way they do

He wrote: "No one knows where and when this dew-like existence
will drop into the grass." (Dogen Zenji)

Kakunen
musho

(on screen)
VAST EMPTINESS
NOTHING HOLY

The fourth dimension: to be attentive to the
infra-ordinary

an intrusion of eternity

"When you see autumn colors,
do not be partial to them.
You should allow the **four** seasons
to advance in one viewing,
and see an ounce and a pound
with an equal eye"
—Dogen zenji

(heard in Japanese, read in English)
(on screen) *"early rice fragrance / pushing through
to right / the 'Rough Sea'"*
—Basho

"The entire world is our mind, the mind of a flower."
(on screen)—Dogen zenji

PART III

JAPAN

Alterity and the Image Effect

"WHY THE FORM COUNTS": OF HOST AND GUEST

with Hiroshi Yoshioka

First published as "On the Fourth Dimension," in English and in Japanese in *Diatxt.* (Kyoto, Japan) Vol. 7, 2002. All rights reserved by Kyoto Art Center.

Yoshioka: *Modern society, especially in Japan, has been obsessed by "speed." This obsession is one with the general tendency of modernity to value speed, but it seems to take an extreme form in this country, as if it were the supreme duty of Japanese modernity to absorb advanced civilization from the outside as quickly as possible, to develop it efficiently inside, and to achieve an industrial success beyond that of the West.*

When I first read your written work, I came across a vision that was opposed to this widespread adoration of speed, convenience, and efficiency. But for you, it seemed to me anyway, it was not a question of simply resisting rationalism and modernity, but of opening a new dimension of reality which can be perceived only when we take the time to think and understand. Or, maybe I just realized the significance of slowness.

When I saw your film The Fourth Dimension *I recalled this earlier impression. With this in mind, could you say something on the subject of "time"? What do you think about this enthusiasm for speed and efficiency which has become more obvious and perhaps oppressive in the digitalized, hyper informational society that we live in today?*

Trinh: Yes, as you put it so nicely, everything boils down to the very simple act of "taking time" to understand, to give and receive. Slowness itself is a modern concept. It is in today's framework of frantic productive activities that "being slow" becomes a problem. Living now in the U.S., what I miss the most from the years I spent in West Africa is the way that time is fully lived there. People's lifestyle in these societies makes it such that "doing nothing" is not only necessary but usually, also very enjoyable. For example, when you come to a friend's house and inquire after him, you'll be told that he's "sitting" in his courtyard, at so's and so's place, or simply "with the men," if it is in a village. There, sitting is an activity of its own, and sitting around by yourself or with others to enjoy the day is a totally "legitimate" occupation.

The African scholar and diviner Malidoma Somé tells of a rather common story about time which I like to recall when I catch myself struggling with a hectic schedule. It's similar to what I've heard in Senegal and also very relevant to the production context of *The Fourth Dimension*. In his village, Somé met with his fellowmen around a calabash of millet beer and told them how such sitting around would be negatively looked upon in the West, whose life pace is much faster. One of the elders asked where these white people run to every morning, and when he was told that they were heading to their workplaces, he asked again: "Why do they have to run to something that is not running away from them?" To which, Somé replied: "They do not have time." Since the word "time" did not exist in his language and he had to use French to express it, the elder went on asking what "time" is; and here their whole conversation came to a halt.

We really think we know time because time is so dominant in our daily activities. But as the laws of science itself reveal, time is as baffling as ever. Somé's anecdote speaks volume for the strangeness of modern life. Not only does "nobody have time" in today's era of global speed (and no one is so poor in time as the one who has forgotten how to live) but it is also true that literally, we cannot have time because we are time. All the motion and commotion we create around ourselves only serves to distract us from this basic reality, which when we do see, we can only see as an irreversible journey from crib to grave. So we are constantly running for fear that if we stop, time may catch up with us. It's only in extreme situations, as with the recent 9/11 event, that suddenly the arrow of time loses its forward-only linearity to take on a multi-spiral course. Once the inner alarm bell starts ringing, the sense of time passing deepens to become much more inclusive. Many people realized then with poignancy that they needed to "slow down" and to take the time to be with themselves and their loved ones.

The Fourth Dimension refers to the dimension of time in cinema; of light—our own light—in spiritual context; and of the unseen within our visible everyday reality. Time, as I lived it during my stay in Japan and as realized in *The Fourth Dimension*, is very precise. As a joke, the length of this digital film is very precisely 86 minutes and 40 seconds. This is the longest length tolerated for mainstream TV broadcasting in the U.S. But being "well aware that television prefers, in any case, programs of half an hour or of less than an hour, I use this TV timeframe simply as an empty ritual. No matter how one may view it, the reality that I present in *The Fourth Dimension* is that of a digitalized Japan. My turning to video in working with Japanese culture is not a mere coincidence. Although cinema is an experience of time and light, digital technology leads us further into an era of intense time. What it offers with high tech machines operating at the speed of light is—the speed-time image.

This is where form and content are one and the same in *The Fourth Dimension*. Speed, mobility and portability are keywords in today's economy of time. They are also, as you've suggested through the notions of convenience and efficiency, what distinguishes Japan's modernity and contributes to the image she projects as a leading global economic power. After all, Japan turned herself modern at extraordinary speed after the Meiji Restoration. My film was not made to attack Japan's modernization or to oppose her dominant trend of Westernization. It would be naïve to forget where

I stand and how my own digital images of Japan are produced for the viewers. (In my productive mobility, I am very much part of the "jet" society and of the "fast species.") Nor was the film made to promote that trend by portraying Japan in her new gadgets and extravaganzas. There's a whole body of films whose images abound in this direction. Mostly shot in Tokyo, these feature the world of technocratic conforming Japan through the robotic, the pornographic, the sensational weird, the synthetic ideal; all yielding to elaborate fantasies of decadent mores and freakish forms of youth social deviance. Such apparent breaking of taboos is after all very safe, very contained and unthreatening; they are part of the forbidden Japan outsiders love to depict, which insiders often happily oblige and perpetuate.

In working not with unmediated Japan, but with the Image of Japan, what seems far more challenging to me is to address the intense, infinite experience of speed within stillness, *and vice-versa*. No opposition, only the containment of one within the other, such as also: the spatial within the temporal; the three times in one: present, past and future; or else, the geophysical time of traveling across Japan within the cinematic time of reassembling and re-traveling in optical speed. These frames of time are rituals proper to new technology. They are precisely what enable us, makers and viewers, to shift the preconceived image of Japan and to play differently with the tension between tradition and modernity; spirituality and technology; inside and outside; host and guest; form and content. Rituals, as expanded in *The Fourth Dimension*, are figures of both conformity and freedom, depending on how one understands and practices them.

Y: *I'm very sympathetic with the perspective of your film, that of locating rites and rituals not only in the obvious places, in festival and ceremonies, but also in everyday life. Your treatment of this aspect of Japanese society is very complex and insightful. Living inside this society, however, I often feel these everyday "rites," which are deeply imbedded in our language, have become binding and repressive. What's worse, people here are seldom aware of them as rites. At the same time, I know it is the unconscious and ritualized nature of our interactions and language that enables us to avoid many of the conflicts that plague other countries. Did you, when you shot this film, have a similar ambivalence about the place of ritual in modern society? And did you change your understanding after you finished the film?*

T: I certainly share your feelings. In *Reassemblage*, a previous film of mine that questions exoticism, Western aid, and the objectifying eye of anthropology, I deliberately avoided focusing on any ritual event while shooting in Senegal. But, as you can see, in *The Fourth Dimension*, the extra-ordinary—festival events, parades, theatrical and musical performances, religious architecture—plays as important a role as the ordinary of daily life. This is partly due to the experience I had during my stay in Japan, which was at the same time very moving and very frustrating. That stay was not the first (I had been in Japan several times before) but it was the longest, since I came as a visiting professor at the Institute for Gender Studies of Ochanomizu University. Both the length and the intensity of the experience allowed me to have a "taste"—a bittersweet one—of the confining nature of Japanese everyday rites and their relentless pressure to conform.

I am thinking here for example, of the importance of such a notion as that of host and guest. My Japanese friends were impeccable hosts—a trait that many foreigners have recognized in the people—and I had greatly benefited from their kindness. But this kindness proved at times to be rather overwhelming. In several incidences during my travel across Japan, I was shocked by the almost obsessive perseverance of my hosts to inquire after my whereabouts and well-being, to track me down scornfully in my wayward itinerary, or to settle once and for all, against my will, where I should be accommodated—even when such decision meant far more trouble for the host. The deep frustration I underwent and the irremediable hurt I caused when I refused to conform were such that I found myself perturbed by what I repeatedly saw as a dramatic ambivalence between care and control.

It took me some time to recognize the fuller significance of acting one's role in society. As one of the statements of the film says: "We are Noh actors moving in the screen space of ritual, ethical life." Rather than persist in asking imperatively whether it is care or control, I had slowly come to understand that it was both care and control. This was the kind of relation one usually only has with one's mother, for example. I was profoundly moved to see how much people took to heart their role as host, while I so reluctantly gave in to my role as a guest. We foreigners like to think of ourselves as mobile—"real," informal and free. We are quick to condemn social rituals as stifling; we refuse to assume our role, we resist our status as outsider, and yet we expect people to treat us immediately as one of theirs—as insiders. In short, we want to bypass the steps and to speed up the process without having to "take the time" to understand in order to shift the boundaries.

A quote of Dogen zenji says in the film: "If you neglect the formality of guest and host, you can understand neither the true nor the phenomenal." The host's generous function, which is to receive and to vouch for the guest's behavior, further gains in dimension when applied to filmmaking: here the medium and the maker are both host and guest to the realities of Japan. If I can't assume the role of a guest, I can't take on the role of a host either. These are heartfelt questions I had to struggle with; they inform the way I critically materialize my encounter with Japanese culture in *The Fourth Dimension*. Two ritualized times run through the length of the film: train time and drum time—the clock of modernity and the beat of tradition. As you've pointed out, language rites act on social relations; the secular, the ceremonial and the sacred are not separable. We can't see into the other face of rituals when we indulge in divisive realities and compartmentalized knowledge. To ignore, to isolate, to naturalize or to take for granted the very rituals that define our activities would amount to letting conformity reign. I prefer, in this film, to feature the interrelated space of ritualization, to hint at the rules at work so as to compose with speed and to experience "why the form counts."

Y: *I was deeply impressed by the selective use of Japanese speech in the film. What was especially interesting for me was the sense that the voices somehow alienated Japanese from the Japanese! It was as if my own language had become a strange piece of music. It reminded me of a conversation I had with a British friend who told me—she was teaching English at school—that her students regarded English as a kind of music, not as* *a language. And indeed, I have often thought of that as our general attitude toward foreign languages in Japan. On the other hand, people believe that one language, their own, must be something special, that there has to be a clear and hard border between Japanese and other languages.*

T: It is most interesting that you bring in the musical dimension of language here. More than visual art, music is said to be the very art form of new generations. Compositions with sound harmonics already constitute models of speed design. I have always emphasized both in my films and in my books that it is through language that one hears the music of a person and of a people. One distinguishes one neighborhood, one town, and one region from another by the sound and rhythm of each location. When I travel, what allows me to recognize where I am across ethnic borders is the intonation of people's vocal interactions. Our language and music are our identity.

The use of Japanese sayings, sentences and words in *The Fourth Dimension* was initially triggered by an encounter with the performer herself. I heard Shoko Hikage's *koto* and vocal performance shortly before the montage of the film, when I went to see a Butoh dance in San Francisco. I was highly inspired, so I ended up asking her to perform (with Greg Goodman) for the film soundtrack. I wanted very much to hear Japanese in *The Fourth Dimension*, rather than simply to understand its meaning. But to invite the viewer to hear it as well, I had to mark it, and hence the need to have it both "ordinarily" spoken and "ritually" performed. I'm reminded here of *gidayu*—this stylized and highly emotive use of the voice common to Japanese music and theater, in which a chanter and a *shamisen* player are usually included. Voice and language are emphatically non-naturalistic in performance. Shoko's vocals play a very important part of the film—one in which I directly appeal to the Japanese-speaking viewer, while offering all viewers another dimension of language.

Poetry—the poetry of one's existence—arises when words are brought back to music. Although my films can all be said to be music of the eye, this one stands out for me both as a spectrum of time and a musical latticework. Japanese language has a wide range of subtle inflections; its sentences can easily eliminate the subject and thrive on ambivalence. Paradoxically, it is by working on its very musical attributes that one marks a language (or a people's identity) in its specificity and at the same time, displaces its rigid codes. In the play between sense and sound, *The Fourth Dimension* weaves a number of different time zones. There is, for example, a dialogue between the stream of *koto* music drifting and swelling with the images, and the stream of narration pensively read in my own voice. In contrast to this English narration's steady excess of sound, thoughts and meanings, the occasional, single Japanese words performed by Hikage powerfully irrupt into the sonorous fabric. They are sound-hieroglyphs that punctuate the film space. Since sounds have their own internal lives, and every word stands by itself as a powerful magnet, it is largely through their interactions that the film comes to life and resonates.

Y: *You were born in Vietnam, spoke French in school, moved to the USA and studied there, taught English in France, and taught music in Senegal. And the many authors who have inspired you also reflect this multiple linguistic/cultural background. In contrast, the majority of Japanese were born into a society which is thought of as strictly* *monocultural and monolingual (though this is not completely true). The theme of this issue, "Lingua Franca," addresses precisely this situation. After living and working in Japan, what is your sense of the Japanese attitude toward the English language or, more generally, to all non-native languages?*

T: One of the first things I noticed while in Japan was the fact that Japanese television, like American television, was predominantly monolingual. Both countries are leading economical powers and both hold on to the myth of their own uniqueness. The more powerful the development of their communication technology, the more isolated they tend to remain from the rest of the world. This also applies to the more dominant cultures of Western Europe—French, English and German. Whereas in other parts of Europe a large number of people do speak more than one language, and in Africa, even villagers in the remote countryside speak fluently three or four African languages. Power relations determine the degree of multilingual-ness of a culture.

This being said, generalizations have their limits and depending on the circumstance, the reverse logic can also apply. There are obviously many more factors involved such as those of privilege, speed and mobility. The relation between Japanese and English is a complex one—as complex, for me, as the political position that Japan maintains toward the United States and the West. It is a love-hate relationship that bears many faces. While mobility and globalization require that one adopt a lingua franca to do outreach work and to expand the horizon of one's activities, it also deepens one's need for singularities in resistance. Here is where specific rites and circumstantial boundaries play an important role, and the tribalism of youth rave culture (which I also show in the film) is an example.

It is not surprising, with this in mind, to see why many people in Japan seem to try very hard to learn English and yet rarely master it. Conscious or unconscious, there is a kind of resistance to this mobile language of commercial exchange and of capitalism, whose power is represented by the U.S. Among the older generations of Japanese, I've met people who happily spoke French but were very reluctant to speak English, although their level of fluency in English was the same or even higher than the one they had in French. And the reason for that, they said, is historical: language is shared, collective memory, and they can't forget what the States had done to Japan. For the younger generations, however, English represents a certain freedom, a license to break from the bounds of norms and conventions. I did notice how the coded tone and register of people's speech drastically drops away when they switch from Japanese to English. It's remarkable: you have a different person in front of you, and this is particularly true with women. English serves as a kind of safety valve, perhaps the way alcohol does for Japanese culture: although one can vent one's frustrations and true feelings, and even carry on outrageously, the excess remains, in the end, coded as it is contained.

I also don't think that because one is raised with only one language, one can only speak one language. Language is not only an exercise of power or of resistance; it is also an act of creativity. Differences developed within the same language can be infinitely rich. In public or working situations, I often felt that although those of us involved all spoke English, we profoundly spoke different languages. Just as you have the local within the global, and vice-versa, you have the vernacular within the vehicular, the alternative within the official, the tribal within the governmental, and so on. In relation

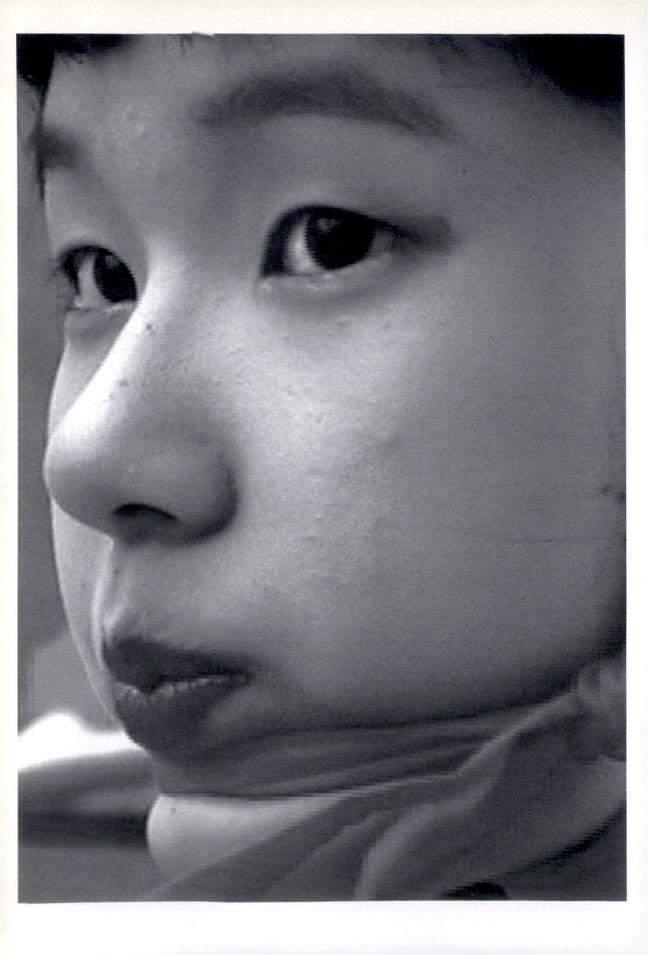

to today's trend of trans-nationality, the revival of the regional can be most reactionary, but as artists, feminists and activists of the diverse diasporas around the world have shown, one has to exile oneself from one's own language, to assume the role of a guest within one's own territory, if one is to create anew and become multilingual within one's own language.

INAPPROPRIATE/D ARTIFICIALITY

with Marina Grzinic

First published as "Shifting the Borders of The Other" trans. into Japanese, *Déjà-vu bis* (Tokyo), No 15, July 1998, 14–15, with the following introduction: *"Trinh T. Minh-ha, the Vietnamese American filmmaker and feminist theorist, is currently living in Tokyo, teaching as Visiting Professor at the Institute for Gender Studies at Ochanomizu University, Tokyo. I have had—due to space restrictions—to cut the long but still, from my point of view, too short interview with Trinh T. Minh-ha, almost into half. I talked with her for about an hour on June 2, 1998 at her temporary office at Ochanomizu University, and I realized I could keep asking her questions and exchange thoughts and doubts with her for hours. Her precise process of selecting terms, expressions, of defining theoretical tools and of clarifying words, statements and thoughts testified, again and again, to her enormous intellectual, artistic and leftist background and the direction of her work."*

Grzinic: *I would like to start the interview by questioning the paradigm, that is the notion of the "inappropriate/d other" that you conceived in the mid-eighties. Is this paradigm still effective, still workable today? If not, how can we grasp the politics of the Other, and who is the Other today?*

Trinh: We can read the term "inappropriate/d other" in both ways, as someone whom you cannot appropriate, and as someone who is inappropriate. Not quite other, not quite the same. Of course, there are many other terms that I've handled similarly in my writings, such as "the moon" or the colors "red" and "gray," for example. Depending on the context, one term may prove to be more relevant than another. In response to your question, I would say certainly, for how can a notion like "the inappropriate/d other" be subject to being effective only at certain times, when its very function is to resist appropriation? It all depends on how the notion is lived and carried on. Since inappropriate(d)ness does not refer to a fixed location, but is constantly changing according to the specific circumstances of each person, event or struggle, it works differently according to the moment and the forces at work. To refer to this situation in which one is always slightly off, and yet not entirely outside, I've also used the term "elsewhere," to which I've added "within here"—an elsewhere within here. That is, while you are entirely involved with the now-and-here, you are also elsewhere, exceeding your limits even as you work intimately with them. This is a dimension that you develop simultaneously, not something that happens linearly and successively in two time-phases, with one coming before the other.

So you can say that within the "inappropriate/d other" are the many different possibilities of other or of otherness I've elaborated in my work. You can never be exhaustive as to who or what the other is. If you try to speak for everybody, what you have to say runs the risk of becoming a mere decoration. To give an example, when Desmond Tutu was visiting the States in the mid-eighties, he gave a speech to a packed audience at the Greek Theater in Berkeley. Before the speech, an entertainer who was trying her best to do something appropriate to Tutu's politics and to fill in the gaps while the audience was waiting asked the audience to sing along with the refrain of the song "We Are The World." Each time the refrain came back, it was comfortably adapted to address, for example, African Americans the first time, Native Americans the next time, and Asian Americans the time after, and so on, until we had covered all the "minorities" groups. Imagine such a chorus. This is decoration. This is how difference becomes harmlessly decorative and how the media conveniently understand political correctness, using it in the name of multiculturalism to degrade multiculturalism.

For me, the question is not to be exhaustive in what one does—this is a mere illusion, because one can never be exhaustive enough—but to provide tools workable across struggles. So that when I use the notion of "the inappropriate/d other" in the very specific contexts of the West's other, and Man's or man's other, I am exploring the question of gender and ethnicity with an eye and an ear that, while not naming all groups, also takes into consideration, for example, the struggle of sexuality. The tools offered can be taken up and used on their own terms, by gays and lesbians, and by those whom society's standards of 'normalcy' have marginalized. You cannot cover all areas, you can only speak in certain specific areas, but you can listen with the ears of other marginalized groups. This is for me infinitely more challenging and important than speaking for everyone or mentioning everyone at the same time. Hence I do not always know who this other is or to whom the term can be fully applied, but the tool provided should be such that it can reach a wider range of peoples, whose struggles link them with other struggles of liberation.

G: *The term can be used therefore in a poetical and a political way?*

T: Certainly.

G: *How much it can be used as a political tool between East and West, Asian and American territory today is a tendency to surpass the gap between these disparate territories, to blur the differences?*

T: When you mentioned East and West, as you are from Slovenia, I immediately thought of the difference between Eastern and Western Europe.

G: *I am using the notion of "inappropriate/d other" in my work for such a distinction, but I would prefer to rethink it in the direction of the difference between Asian and North American spaces, as you were born in Vietnam, but you live in the USA and we are now discussing the "inappropriate/d other" here in Tokyo.*

T: I would say that even though I come from Vietnam—and whether I want it or not, I certainly do belong to this whole context of Asia whose cultural heritages cut across national borderlines—I don't see my location as being primarily Asian or American. There are so many ways to situate oneself and to determine our alliances. I spent some of the most important years of my life in West Africa, for example, and I was strongly politicized by African and North African contexts. Living in the States has also, from the very beginning, sensitized me to the struggles of Black people and of Native Americans. So when I speak of the other of the West, it is never only Asia. Within the Asian communities, if you speak to Chinese or to Japanese people, for example, what they know about Vietnamese culture is likely to be less widespread than, let's say, what the Vietnamese know about Chinese and Japanese cultures. The "minorities" are always socialized to see more than one point of view. So my positioning in relation to Asia and within the Asian community is already slightly off and different. The tendency to locate me within a geographically specific fight—whether in Vietnam, in Asia or in the States—can be very confining and reductive. Even when I was directly asked by governmental representatives of Vietnam at international events, "How do you think you can be useful to your country?" I could only reply by saying I hoped I could be useful, not merely to the Vietnamese community—even though I would be most happy if the tools I devised could serve this community—but to a larger context of Third World non-alignment or of hybridity in the diaspora. This is just a clarification that is not meant to deflect what you have asked.

How does one situate—politically and culturally—Vietnam, China or Japan, for example? Japan is certainly not a country that fits the general definition of the Third World, even though in certain situations in the West, the Japanese have been treated as members of the Third World. No doubt, what has historically happened to Japanese immigrants in the States shows that through racial discrimination, they belong among all the other Third World peoples, even though economically Japan, as a global power, stands apart from the block of Third World nations. This is already one example of inappropriateness.

Vietnam, on the other hand, has also historically undergone a short period of Japanese take over. And yet to a certain extent Japanese, unlike Chinese people, have always stood out (in our eyes) as the people whose work ethic and discipline we praise. What I heard during my childhood in relation to the Japanese, aside from the war atrocities, often concerned their ability to appropriate the tools of the dominant masterfully and to combine German discipline and precision with a family-based work ethic. Japanese products have been highly rated all over the world. This is something that many of us Vietnamese speak about admiringly at the same time as we tend to dismiss it, precisely because of the disciplinary aspect involved.

Here, rather than simply condemn or admire such a discipline, one can see Japan strategically in terms of its slight "inappropriate(d)ness" with regard to its positioning in the divide between First World and Third World, or between tradition and modernity.

Certainly, the other aspect of Japanese culture that seems to stand out most prominently for outsiders is the persistent perpetuation of certain traditional cultural aspects in the midst of high technology. This can be another form of inappropriate(d)ness. I am not talking here about the imitation or simple preservation of an objectified past reality but rather, about something that goes on living both in straight traditional appearances and in modulated transformations. Such a practice, which China, for example, has attempted to readapt, not without great difficulty, in the aftermath of the Cultural revolution, is usually carried out in all discrepancies and inconsistencies in other non-Western contexts.

Whereas in Japan that spirit of "coexistence" seems to circulate in the details of everyday life, even if these details may be today emptied of spiritual dimension. What I first saw on the TV monitor of the airplane when landing in Japan was the ground traffic controller who directed the plane with precise gestures to its assigned place, and who bowed to the plane as he completed his job. Such a bow may appear utterly banal to the insider, but for me it is a sign that remains telling as to one's attitude toward the world. The sense of interbeing and of transience in this human, animal and mineral world is very much alive. Foreigners overwhelmed by the abundance of street activities and displays in Tokyo have also time and again spoken of the Edo spirit breathing on in modern times. What I've just said in relation to Vietnam, China and Japan are mere generalities that can always be contested in the details. But, what is suggested is that the relation to tradition needs not be one of mere imitation or appropriation, it can be one of transformation and of creativity. You always have to walk this precarious line of difference and of "inappropriate(d)ness" if you are to avoid merely retrieving or rejecting the past.

G: *Although I would like to continue to talk about Japan, let's reflect a little bit more on this difference between us and the other. What are the strategies for locating the difference/s?*

T: One strategical definition of "the inappropriate/d other" I gave in my book, in the context of gender and ethnicity, is that you always fare with at least four simultaneous gestures: that of affirming "I am like you" while persisting in one's difference; and that of insisting "I am different" while unsettling all definitions and practices of otherness arrived at. This is where "inappropriate(d)ness" takes form. Because when you talk about difference, there are many ways to take it in; if you simply understand it as a division between cultures, between people, between entities, you can't go very far with it. But when that difference between entities is being worked out as a difference also within, things start opening up. Inside and outside are both expanded. Within each entity, there is a vast field and within each self is a multiplicity.

G: *How much do modern technology and cyberspace as a corporate constructed else-where, along with the myth of globalization contribute today to the construction of this difference or in blurring its boundaries?*

T: It all depends on how technology is being developed and in what direction it is being geared. I've written at length about the aesthetic of objectivity and the pursuit of naturalism in the development of a media technology that promotes increasing unmediated access to reality. The aim is naively to render the tools and relations of production more and more transparent, or to come closer to truth with each step taken by limiting reality to what is immediately visible while making recording devices as invisible as possible.

Today's computer technology may be more "realistic" in its challenge of the "real" but we can say, with Paul Virilio, that what we are facing in cyberworld is a different kind of colonization. Instead of colonizing by force territories exterior to our own, we are now colonizing and being colonized through monitors and passwords within our own territories. The technology that is being perfected continues to be geared toward economic ends and to serve the marketing mind that controls today's societies. If technology is in the hands of philosophers, activists or artists, for example, its function and direction can be very different. It can be another creative tool rather than being a coded and coding tool through which the standardization of communication (with ever greater speed and accessibility) is maximized despite the impressive proliferation of choices devised.

I am glad you mentioned the blurring of boundaries and differences in relation to cyberspace. Yes, there's a lot of talk about blurred boundaries or about a "borderless world" that seem to partake in such a corporate mentality. For me, the question of hybridity or of cultural difference has never been a question of blurred boundaries. We constantly devise boundaries, but these boundaries, which are political, strategical or tactical—whatever the circumstance requires, and each circumstance generates a different kind of boundary—need not be taken as ends in themselves. The notion of the migrant self, which has taken on a new lease in our times, is very relevant here. The self-in-displacement or the self-in-creation is one through which changes and discontinuities are accounted for in the making and unmaking of identity, and for which you need specific, but mobile, boundaries. For example, when do you call yourself a feminist, when you do not call yourself a feminist, when do you see yourself as part of the East, and when do you when you tell people the West is also in me? When I am speaking about the West I am not speaking about a reality outside myself. It is not a question of blurring boundaries or of rendering them invisible. It is a question of shifting them as soon as they tend to become ending lines.

G: *How much are we, as artists using technology and producing films, photographs or digitals images, part of the system of corporate production of the myth of total visibility?*

T: Producing within these different areas of image-making means that what we come up with remains specific to each of our locations and of the media at work. So what I do may not fully apply to other people's contexts. As you've said, we are part of this whole system of media production and media visibility, and in the films I have made, there are many ways to work creatively with it and despite it when you walk the edge of not quite staying inside it and not quite standing outside it. There's no "pure" ground from which I can voice criticism of the media, even if I resist the marketing mind and operate in a venue that is not commercial.

With the tools available, you can create different time-spaces that expose or turn to advantage the fissures, gaps and lapses of the system. We're coming back here to the notion of inappropriate(d)ness as linked to the notion of boundary event, which I've been elaborating in my more recent works. The challenge is not to fall prey to the

THE FOURTH DIMENSION

dominant process of totalization: rather than working at bringing, through gradual acquisition, what has been kept invisible into visibility, you would have to break with such a system of dualities and show, for example, what constitutes invisibility itself as well as what exceeds mere visibility.

G: *So it is a matter of constant positioning and this is a thoroughly artificial process. Moreover, can we also see that today the mainstream is using similar strategies to the ones used by experimental productions?*

T: I will take a detour here to respond to the term "artificial." In certain intellectual milieus it is very difficult to talk about the "spiritual" without immediately raising suspicion. But since I work with resonances in displacement, I would ask, for example, what is artificiality in the context of spirituality? When you mentioned positioning as an artificial process, I immediately say yes, not because "artifice" connotes something not true or not real, but because the world caught in its life and death processes can be seen entirely in term of artifice and artificiality. In other words, the world is a "radical illusion"—to use a term that artificially links Baudrillard to Buddhist thought. When one says everything man-made is all artificial, one is not necessarily implying that nature is truer. For ultimately, it is in producing the artificial that one makes "truth" apparent and gives shape to one's situation.

You also mentioned the tendency of the mainstream to appropriate experimental tools. In fact, what they can appropriate is only an instrument or a technique. Here I am making a difference between "tool" and "instrument." Let's say that the function of an instrument is to serve—a message, an idea, an activity, a purpose—whereas the function of a tool is to give form, to de-form and to trans-form. We don't even know what idea that creative tool will lead to. And ideas may serve but they also act on material and mental realities. If the mainstream uses strategies similar to those of experimental productions, it uses them toward totally different ends. Its aim is to reify for consumerist purposes, so it reproduces what at first sight may appear similar; but missing the spirit of "purposefully purposeless" experimentation, it turns everything into a matter of techniques in the process of totalizing meaning. Such artificiality is to be distinguished from the artificiality I elaborated earlier, in which everything caught in the cycle of visibility and invisibility or of life and death is artificial, including our own bodies, our existences. Nothing is "natural" in the usual sense of the term. Perhaps the only "natural" element or event is this energy, this force that exists in no single material form, but thanks to which things materialize, take form, mutate and disintegrate.

TRAVELING (IN) TIME

with Irina Leimbacher

This article first appeared in the March 2001 issue of *ReleasePrint*, the magazine of Film Arts Foundation.

Leimbacher: *In describing your new piece you've pointed out how today, when one goes on a journey, travel is ritualized through the visual machine. Could you speak about* The Fourth Dimension *and how it embodies or engages with that idea of a ritualized journey?*

Trinh: It's important that we understand the word 'ritual' in its larger sense. The term usually refers to a coded social performance such as a ceremonial practice established by tradition or a religious service of a prescribed order. Japanese culture certainly abounds with such codified practices that can be very confining to both outsiders and insiders. But that's only one dimension of the ritual. Making a video, for example, is to engage in ritual—both the rituals of new technologies and those of creating and structuring images. Traveling in a country and showing its culture is another form of ritual. The journey here is both physical and spiritual. It involves the initial material time of physical displacement from one specific place to another in Japan as well as the immaterial time of instantaneous remote control generated in video framing and viewing. In other words, rituals serve as a 'frame' whose stabilizing effect, experienced through repetition in cycles and in rhythmic recurrences, allows us to see things with a different intensity and, as stated in *The Fourth Dimension*, to perceive the ordinary in an extra-ordinary way.

Of course, in a society that thrives on media images, before we even leave for a journey we are already exposed to a swarm of preset visuals that are bound to condition the way we see Japan. We organize our travel and ritualize our itineraries according to what the visual machine promotes. So to enter *The Fourth Dimension* is to recognize the multiplicity of times at work in any single moment of the journey, and to fare at the edge of what appear as both confining and expansive in the rituals of images.

L: *How often were you in Japan?*

T: This was my fifth time in Japan. Before that, I had been invited there to tour with my films, to serve on festival juries, to speak at retrospectives of my work in Tokyo or to give lectures at conferences. During the last stay, I taught for a semester at the Center for Gender Studies of Ochanomizu University. I had then another project in mind—the fiction film I'm working on now—and I was trying to fundraise. It was while doing research for that film that I shot all the footage that led to *The Fourth Dimension*.

L: *I believe this is your first piece in digital video after years of working in 16mm and 35mm film. What was it like for you working in video?*

T: After *A Tale of Love*, which was shot in 35mm, I found myself in such debt (laughs) that it took me a while to recover from that. So I told myself that the next project should be a very intimate one in which I do most of the work myself, like with *Reassemblage*. I also thought that the time was ripe for me to learn more about the potentials of video and its properties, and to get involved in digital technology. For that, I had to learn everything from zero so as to be able to work more intimately with the medium, in my own pace and with my own demands for experimentation. One can always work with someone knowledgeable and expand one's mind, but when you experiment intimately with a medium, you develop a very specific relationship with it—one that grows with you and isn't possible to teach nor to transfer on to another person.

In my experience of the video world—which is rather limited—I would say that I don't find the same spirit of disinterested camaraderie as in the independent filmmaking world. When I came into film I benefited from the assistance of very dedicated film people who did not hesitate to give help and guidance, and who took pleasure in doing this. I would always remember with much affection how Debbie Meehan, a filmmaker who now lives in New York, introduced me to the crafts of filmmaking. Thanks to her and Charlie Woodman, her assistant, I learnt filmmaking from A to Z, including negative cutting—for nothing. We were just exchanging and passing on skills. This is something that I haven't encountered in the video world. Those working in this world with a great heart and a long-lasting commitment to the 'independent' community have all been working extensively with film (like Gary Coates who did the color timing for my video at Western Images). It seems as if the video world is primarily a world of huge solitaries (laughs); people who easily tune in with the way the computer mind works, quickly learn an area of video technology and claim it as their area of expertise. So you can become an 'expert' in very little time, and you put all your effort in fortifying that expertise. Whenever questions are asked that happen to cross the demarcation of a territory, a wall immediately arises as one is promptly sent to other experts' whereabouts.

With the marketing mind controlling new technologies, rather than seeing tools made more convivial, what we often witness is the multiplication of experts and expertises. The multiplication of videomakers is very different from the multiplication of experts in video, and in the latter, what gets refined is but the compartmentalization of knowledge, albeit in a proliferation of choices.

L: *So will you work in video again, either shooting or editing digitally.*

T: I don't have much of a choice here . . .

L: *Your flatbed is long gone?*

T: No I still have it, but I will probably have to sell it. I have no choice because the funding venues for the media arts in the States are really depressing. Once you have received a grant from an organization you usually can't apply for it again. It takes much more time to fundraise than to make a film. For each feature-length film that takes me one year to complete, for example, I spend three or four years fundraising. There are two categories of filmmakers for whom it's very difficult to get funds: the emerging ones who haven't done enough to "prove" their worth, and the enduring ones who have done a body of non-commercial work. Everybody thinks ok, she can find funding somewhere else, and then you just get stuck. I hear similar observations from some of my friends, like Yvonne Rainer, who has the same problem. Because, even though we have a body of work, our work hasn't gone mainstream.; it survives on the support of neither the film industry nor the television network. It's very difficult.

L: *I wanted to ask you about your play with framing in the film, and the use of digital effects to create moving frames within the frame. The opening section with the highway in fog moving across the frame is exquisitely beautiful. You also sometimes put color on parts of the image. Could you speak about those types of manipulations?*

T: Well, one aspect of Japanese culture for which video seems to be the ideal tool to portray is precisely this mobility and multiplicity of framing. Working with multiple framings in a shot is made much easier with digital technology and the indefinite possibilities of layering images and sound. One of the very strong experiences I had in Japan was the way doors and openings are devised. You come to someone's home and they invite you to sit down. As they start airing the room and opening it wider to the view outside, they proceed to slide the partition doors in intricate shifts of rights and lefts and middles, and there, shuttling in front of you are at least four or five framings of the outdoor garden. Or, you go to the toilet in an older house in the countryside. If you stand up you have one kind of framing, one kind of view, and if you sit down you have another [laughs]. It was this kind of multiplicity of framing that I wished to recreate in the work as related to the culture.

Unfortunately when I was first exploring this on video, the only thing people more experienced with the medium could come up with are a few preset video effects that look contrived and uninteresting—a mere effect for effect's sake. It's a real challenge because you can't imitate, you have to create in context. In the opening passage you mention, viewers have seen a traveling framing within a frame, a kind of floating image whose trajectory delimits the screen space, a play between the highway and the "light-way," or even a link with film through the panoramic image. There's an invitation at the outset to see something else than the mere content of the image: as with the art of packaging in Japan, the gift is not necessarily in what the package contains, but in the precision of the folds and the lines of the packaging itself. There's a sense that when

you look at an image, it is always an image within another image, an image that leads elsewhere.

L: *Sound has always played a very significant role in your work, and I know that you are a composer with a background in ethnomusicology. The soundtrack of* The Fourth Dimension *is stunning, interweaving a variety of location sounds with a score by* The Construction of Ruins *and your voiceover. Could you speak about your work with the composers and your experience overall designing the sound?*

T: We work with a situation in which I can say there's no composer per se. We are (the two musicians and I) all composers. Very often people ask me why I don't compose for my films. But when you work with a culture, rather than composing from nowhere or from your own background, it's better to compose with the sound you encounter in that culture. So the notion of the composer is here already displaced and decentralized. And this is where the Construction of Ruins, represented by Greg Goodman, takes on an important role in my films. Greg plays the "prepared piano" (to use a Cagean term), which he prefers to call the "unprepared piano" since he does improvisation with all kinds of "unwanted objects." The other musician, Shoko Hikage is a Japanese koto player and a vocalist who also excels in improvisation, so it was easy to have them play together with no rehearsals. Since I myself compose music, I don't really need a score for the films. What is essential in the way we, performers and director/editor, work together is the intense listening that determines the shaping of the music.

I remember when I was working on *A Tale of Love* at the Fantasy Building, the sound mix for a big production was going on and I was told that it was the thirteenth mix that they had done by then because the director was not happy with the score composed for his film. This tells us a lot about the way film music is created and about the hierachy that exists between ear and eye. Their relationship continues to be one of domination and subordination. In the editing process you have the image that comes first and then the musician composes the score for the image. The function of the soundtrack is mainly that of illustrating and *underscoring* the visuals. Whereas in my practice, you have the same "rawness" in the visual footage as in the sound recorded when you come to the editing table: Both are given the same importance as sometimes it is the image that determines the cut and othertimes it is the sound that dictates the unfolding of images. This process allows me to work with sound intimately and in a lively way—I can punctuate with utmost precision, go back and forth, change intervals, create silence, rephrase and repeat as desired. In brief, you can compose along while you are editing. This is where digital technology is at its best as the possibilities it opens up with indefinite layering and molding of sound have been most exciting to me in the process of making *The Fourth Dimension.* There's no need to write and rewrite the score. Greg and Shoko played for a whole afternoon, they just improvised, and sometimes I would give an initial mood or an initial image, and from there they would plunge ahead.

L: *So they would look at one image?*

T: No, they were not looking at anything, I just gave them a mental image or suggested a specific move or a mood, and they would improvise from there. And in improvisation

each sound released as in a throw of dice determines how the players would interact with one another, and the session was really intense. So, what you have in my films and video is never a homogenized space of sight and sound, but always a heterogeneous space between ear and eye as enriched by the multiplicity of elements involved.

L: *How long did you work on interweaving sound and image?*

T: The whole editing took me over three months (although the preparation for it took several more months). Because the shooting was done initially for research purpose, I had a huge amount of material to sort out.

L: *That seems short given the complexity of the piece.*

T: [Laughs] Yes, one really has to stay with it and work with it very intensely.

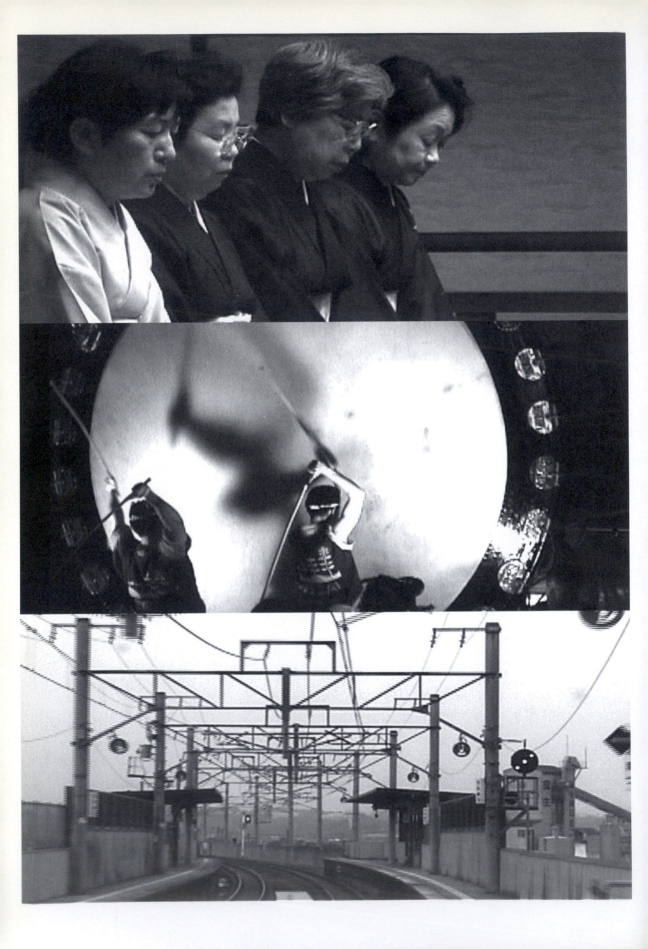

THE DOOR OF RHYTHM

with Kazuko Takemura

First published in *Image Forum* (contemporary art and film journal, Tokyo, Japan), Vol. 1, No. 0, Spring 1999.

Takemura: *First of all, I'd like to say a little about the aim of our interview, or about what kind of questions we want to ask you today and why. As you know, this interview will appear in the first renewal number of Image Forum, which will start again this autumn after two year suspension of publication. This magazine is published by Image Forum as a specific film journal mainly for readers such as film critics, film makers or younger people who want to make films or people who are specifically interested in films.*

But at the same time, the editors hope to make the renewal magazine not a specific technical journal in a narrow sense, but a journal which can somewhat introduce the readers to contemporary cultural events through films, which means, to provide some information about what is going on in the culture or society within and outside this country. And they are planning to make an internet version of this magazine as well so that more people can have access to this publication or this journal. In this sense, the magazine itself will be a cultural event, maybe this is the editor's hope, I've heard.

And Minh-ha, you have already been introduced to the Japanese people. Two of your books were translated into Japanese and all of your films have already been shown in the theater of Image Forum and in several film festivals. And a lot of people came to your lectures at Ochanomizu University or at various occasions held this summer in Tokyo and Kyoto. In the symposium held two years ago at the Tokyo Metropolitan Museum of Photography, a number of people—over the capacity of the hall—came there and some of them who listened to your speech were sitting on the floor.

But we must say, the readers and audience are still limited to the academic world or film experts, owing to the limited chances of screening of your films in Japan and partly to the prevailing discourse that your works, both films and writings, are difficult, that is, academic, technical, or experimental to the general audience. I don't think so. Your works, for instance Surname Viet Given Name Nam *and* Reassemblage *are strongly movies and the colors of* A Tale of Love *are very beautiful. Your book,* Woman, Native, Other *is very impressive to young people: my undergraduate students as well as graduate students came to my office and speak in glowing terms as to how moved they are by your book. But anyway, there is a fact that your audience and readers are still limited, so far, unfortunately.*

So by this interview, I'd liked more people to know about you. I hope this interview to be a kind of introduction for people who have not had any opportunities of access to your films or your books, and at the same time to provide a new perspective or a new point of view, for those people who have already seen or read your work in some way, by asking you about your various experiences before and during your work on films and writings.

Trinh: To begin with the question of audience, when someone says my work is difficult, there may be a number of reasons involved; but let's say that in general, this is not an unusual thing for an artist to hear. Innovative works across generations and geographies are likely to solicit this kind of response, precisely from entrenched academic and experts' milieus. Such an opinion tells us at least as much about the person who voices it as about the artist's work. When you read a poem, for example, you read it differently than when you read a news report. The pace, the expectation, the relation to language cannot be the same. So if you try to read a poem the way you read the newspaper, obviously the poem is difficult. I'm saying this because it's also not unusual for me to meet people from these audiences who have very little education and who, in their own way, understand the work so well.

KT: *Yeah, directly. Maybe academic prejudices prevent them from appreciating your works as they are, I think. But there are many ways to access to your work. Now, let me start with the questions about your younger days. You are born and brought up in Vietnam and went to the United States to study English literature? At a university?*

T: No, I had a double major: music composition and literature.

KT: *Literature in general?*

T: No, Comparative Literature. Mainly English, American, French, and Francophone literatures.

KT: *My question is why you chose the United States as a place for your study, and why you wanted to study comparative literature, because in Vietnam it seems to me French influence was still strong in those days. And, judging from your writings, you are very influenced by French thinkers and writers such as Roland Barthes, Marguerite Duras, and Cixous. You often mention these writers in your books and articles.*

T: Writers I like are not only in literature, they are often those who cut across many disciplines, such as Deleuze, Derrida, or Benjamin. And further, with a closer look, they are not quite "French." Foucault, for example, lived and taught outside of France for a period of his life. Derrida, like Cixous, grew up in Algeria, and Duras, in Vietnam. Deleuze worked in the margins of his own fields of strength; he was "a strange philosopher" as some of his peers called him. This may answer why, instead of going to France—which would have been only a small change from Vietnam—I preferred to go somewhere else, such as the States.

KT: *In those days you felt as if America could provide you with the freedom of thought or freedom of life?*

T: It's a long story. But let's say it was less a choice than a matter of circumstances. I was not thinking of America in particular; I was just hoping to have an education elsewhere than in Vietnam.

KT: *So, that's why you . . .*

T: Yes, that's why I also went to Africa, and before that, why Francophone African and North African literatures appealed to me.

KT: *In the 70s when you were studying in the United States, deconstruction was flourishing in American academicism, especially in the field of Comparative literature and English literature, I think. But afterwards deconstruction was criticized for its unpoliticalness. It was said that its approach ignores the political phases of literature and criticism, being deeply involved in the minute analyses of literary texts. But in the late 80s new historicism appeared, and since then, the literary canon has been revisioned or rethought and colonialism and the position of women of color have come to be discussed more widely and deeply. Your book* Woman, Native, Other *was completed in the early 80s, despite the fact that it was not published until 1989, so it seems you had already established your critical position as early as the late 70s. Is there any relationship between your critical positioning and the education you received at an American university in the 70s—or a kind of disappointment with it?*

T: The last part of the question sounds more apt. What I have learned during these years can be located somewhere outside, as well as inside, the university but certainly not in the classrooms, except perhaps for one or two professors who encouraged me in my itinerary. Although the book I wrote then (in 1977), *Un art sans oeuvre*, discussed Derrida's work, it did not focus on deconstruction *per se*. I was more interested in anonymity—a concept of non-individualistic subjectivity that involves all at once the works of Artaud, Derrida, Thich Nhat Hanh, John Cage, Daniel Buren, Andy Warhol, Marcel Duchamp, Tristan Tzara, and Stephane Mallarmé. Here is where philosophers, poets, musicians, artists, and Zen activists meet. I cannot say that Derrida's work was popular then; it was rather in the 80s that deconstruction became more widespread among academics.

KT: *I think deconstruction was first introduced in the United States in 1969 or 68? But it is another matter . . .*

T: Yes, when it was introduced and when it became more widespread are two different things . . .

KT: *Yes, they are. Related to this question, you went to France after that to study for one or two years?*

T: No, after that I went to Senegal in Africa. But before I finished my university education in the States, I did go to France for a year, as an exchange instructor. I was teaching English to French students in a lycée.

KT: *You taught English to French people? Why did you decide to go to France? Earlier you said that you wanted to put yourself away from French connection?*

T: The fact that you do not wish to pursue your entire university education under the French system does not mean that you should shut yourself off from anything that has to do with French culture and people. I went there in a one-year exchange program as an instructor, and I did take advantage of the opportunity to take courses at the Sorbonne, in ethnomusicology and also in French southern minority literature (Langue d'Oc). A change in your regular course of activities is always welcome and that trip was an opportunity to go somewhere else to teach.

KT: *Do you have any impressions, or how do you feel the differences between studying in the United States and teaching in France or in terms of academicism?*

T: In my own experience, the French system can be said to be very good from elementary school to the end of high school; but their university system is really stuffy and profoundly hierarchical. Friends of mine who belong to it say that in this system the number of years you have to spend before the obtainment of a degree is all fixed; as long as you observe the norms and the protocol, and you work at climbing the ladder diligently step by step, everything will go smoothly as foreseen. The May 68 events in France resulted from the students' general dissatisfaction with such a system of education . . . I think the university system works much better in the States despite the fact that academic life is also very confining here. But in this system, the gaps and cracks are numerous; there's room for whoever is capable to leap ahead and to climb more than one step at a time. For example, by taking on extra units, I was able to finish my Ph.D. at the age of 24; I would certainly not have been able to do that in the French system.

KT: *It seems that all my previous questions focused upon the geographical dimension, but the next question also concerns a place, Africa, or the days you spent in Africa. Why did you decide to go to Senegal, and what kind of experiences did you have there? I don't mean factual experiences but internal ones. For, both in your writings and in your films, you tried to avoid seeing "other" cultures with objectified camera eyes or with the colonizer's eyes of authority. In Africa you taught music to the people there and generally, teachers are regarded as people of power and knowledge. What of kind of experiences did you have while teaching as a woman of color born in Asia and educated in the 1st and 2nd cultures or countries? In a previous interview you said that in Africa you were taught much more than you taught. In what sense did you say this?*

T: There's no safe ground to stand on here; what is being questioned applies to all realms of your activities. Teaching can be a way of endorsing or of questioning a position of power, which in this case involves a whole set of issues specific to the way you conceive of education. It is by putting such a position on trial, whether in the work of a teacher or in the work of a filmmaker, that I have come up with the books and films you mentioned. Aside from the fact that, as in Foucault's strong distinction, not all relations of power are negative—and relations between parents and children, or between teachers and students, which he considered to be necessary, are here an example—whether or

not these relations become abusive would have to depend on how we teach and how we learn. We have discussed this at the seminars I gave at Ochanomizu, and the scope can be wide-reaching, as the questioning of power in this case implies nothing less than a rethinking of our system of education—how knowledge is transmitted and received, how we define our roles which tend to become fixed and how we can break with the circular relation of supplier and consumer between students and teachers.

The first year I taught at the Dakar Conservatory of Music, I was given students who were very advanced; they were graduating seniors who were themselves becoming music teachers. But what I offered them had not much to do with the classical Western music in which they were trained; I introduced them both to traditional non-western music and to post-Schoenberg experimental music, and we dealt with very fundamental questions that concerned the nature, definitions, boundaries, and systems of notation of music. How do we listen to sound? What do we hear? And if every object has a sound and a vibration of its own, where is the line between music and noise, as Western conventions have it? By asking these questions with my students, I have both awakened them to their own sound environment and learned to listen more attentively to African music myself. Also, while teaching, I took lessons to play the Kora, a twenty-six-string instrument. My teaching was not well received by the directors of the Conservatory, who were greatly alarmed by what they saw as my "destroying what they had carefully taught the students during their four to six years of training." But the students themselves got all excited. Some of them whom I met again a couple years later, told me that what they could never forget of the course was how they had come to hear music, not merely as specialized knowledge, but as a coming to life of a person, an object, or an event. They said that depending on how and where contact is made with an object, it would emit a sound of its own accordingly. In other words, music is in the way reality speaks to them in its everyday sounds.

What I opened up for my students was something they had always had already, but were simply not attentive to in ways that could change their daily life. But I could only teach such courses during the first year at the Conservatory, partly because I met with difficulties with the administration, and more importantly, because in West Africa, the system of education is heavily based on the pre-'68 French model, which means that if you don't teach in accordance with the program that has already been set, with its definite packages of quantified knowledge at each step of the ladder, your students would suffer at the end of year since they would be graded in their yearly examination not by their teachers, but impersonally, by an assigned committee of jurors. So I had to quit teaching there after three years.

KT: *The days in Africa served as a catalyst for you, didn't they? I'd like to ask you how you felt teaching as a woman who came from a developed country. I don't know much about Senegal but in Africa, I think Muslim has influenced gender relationships in a different way than in Christian culture or Buddhist Asian culture. There seems to be a strong controversy between feminists in the First World and feminists in the Third World, specifically in terms of F.G.M (female genital mutilation). Did you have a kind of shock of recognition in Africa? In Africa, I suppose you might strongly have felt yourself being hybrid: a lot of cultures—Muslim, Christianity, Buddhism and Confucianism—came together in you. I'm curious about your feelings or daily feelings there . . .*

T: It was a very difficult situation. Although I would say that I am a hybrid anywhere I go, the experience of belonging nowhere became very concrete during the years I spent in Senegal. In legal terms for example, I don't know where I belong; when paperwork pertaining to my identity and competence was required, I did not know where to go; to the Vietnamese, French, or American Embassy? I had American degrees but was of Vietnamese nationality; I spoke French, had a primary and secondary education based on the French model, and had briefly taught in France, but I was considered American in my education; and on top of it all, I was applying for teaching jobs in a system where most faculty and staff members were only familiar with French education and degrees; so none of the embassies recognized me as truly theirs, and none were willing to issue the documents required.

Anything having to do with my citizenship or legal identity was a huge problem then. But in terms of culture and gender, I partly answered the question when I discussed the position of a teacher earlier. Again, it was because of my privileged position both as outsider coming from the States and as insider coming from another culture colonized by the French, that I have put myself and the subject's representative space on trial the way I did in my work. As for the situation of foreign teachers in Senegal, although I did get a lot of the usual sexual hassles from the male faculty and administrative staff, on the students' side I did not feel discriminated against the way I often do, for example, with students in the States—at least in the few first encounters. Because of who I am and how I look, these often adopt an attitude of testing to see what, really, I am able to teach them as a woman. Whereas in Senegal, there is a much more immediate contact, and I did not have to go through this "testing" phase of rejection and acceptance.

KT: *The reason I ask this question is that the part in which you speak about the alignment of women in* Woman, Native, Other *is most impressive to me. You say the alignment of women is sometimes dangerous because when the category of women is claimed, marginal women of color or women of lower class are displaced or neglected within feminism itself, or when women in the margins try to think of themselves as being at the center and to disguise themselves as dominant English-speaking people. You introduced the episode of the Japanese American writer Mitsue Yamada. So the general category of women is very dangerous. At present most feminists seem to think that way, but in the early 80s or late 70s they did not recognize this danger or this internal repression of feminism I think. I guess your experiences have already led you, as early as in those days in Africa, to this kind of critical position.*

T: They did contribute, but it was only after I left Africa that I focused on the works of women of color in the United States. The situation of African women is somewhat different because when you live in your own country, you are not living as a racial minority, even though you are marginalized as a culture by the European colonizer's culture. My being engaged in the works of women of color in the States was a move I deliberately made in writing *Woman, Native, Other*, because I did not want to engage with what I was previously familiar with, that is, with a body of American, European or Vietnamese writing. I wanted then to leave behind much of the academic luggage I had acquired, and whatever Africa has given me works, not directly but indirectly, in the book.

KT: *So far, in all of your works, both writing and films, except for your first book* Un art sans oeuvre, *English language is used as the means of communication. Of course in* Surname Viet Given Name Nam *you don't treat English as a neutral or natural language of the characters in the film, but rather you call into question the neutrality of language itself, the problematics or new possibilities of translation. In an essay you wrote, you directly discuss the meaning of translation, referring to Walter Benjamin. Could you speak about what language means to you? Language here does not include music or body language, but only language itself in a literal sense.*

T: Verbal language? Rather than answering what language means, I would rather touch on our relationship to language, on the impossibility of an original language in creating, or on the illusion of a universal language of representation in mediating. These are all questions dealt with at length in my films and books. Thinkers of our times have extensively contributed—whether through the feminist struggle, through Lacanian analysis, or through deconstructive, postmodern and postcolonial practices—to our understanding of the social position and workings of language.

People who don't recognize the extent to which language defines us socially and politically and who constantly dismiss it in their invocation of "hard realities" are the very people who take language too seriously and depend too much on it to be able to pull out of it in their speech. Some of the common expressions we often hear are, for example, "this is mere rhetoric" or "this is style, not substance." Such conventional statements are academicism at its worst disguised as common sense; it is to be found as much among academics as among people of other contexts. We think we can simply manipulate language to oppress others or to empower ourselves, but language also exerts its power to enslave us further. The way we use it exposes us in our social conditioning and shows how we can remain mere pawns in the game of power unless we learn to see language as a complex reality of its own; one that we can act on as it acts on us. In other words, language tells our stories as we use it to sustain our fictions.

KT: *My next question concerns the relationship between filmmaking and writing. In 1982 you made your first film called* Reassemblage *and you seemed to have completed your book* Woman, Native, Other *around that time. This mean, I think, that you were then working both on writing and filmmaking. Also after that, it is not that you switched from writing to filmmaking, or vice versa, but you seemed to be working on both simultaneously. Is filmmaking different from writing to you, or are they complementary to each other, which means you use the film medium to say what you cannot convey in writing? I stressed the verbal dimension of language in the last question but this time the definition of language should be expanded to include music communication or visionary messages.*

T: In fact, *Reassemblage* was shot a year before I started writing *Woman, Native, Other,* but it doesn't matter. I mean the linear concept of time doesn't matter, it's quite apt to say that the two projects are linked. But I would not say that my films and books are complementary, because I feel that each one of them is an independent work, and their relationship is rather one of supplementarity—supplement here meaning not just something that you add on, but something that remains independent while also mutually adding to one another.

Some people come to my film work first, then they discover the books afterwards; and some others read the books first, then they see the films; but it doesn't cross my mind to use one in order to serve the other. And certainly, they don't depend on each other to exist. Each creative tool, each medium has its own questions to raise. Depending on the circumstances, I will write or I will make a film. It's not that I will switch from one to the other because I can say what I want to say in one medium and not in the other. Rather, what I can say in this medium, I can also, but differently, say in other media. They stand as a tightly related multiplicity and constitute a body of work, in which each has something similar and different to offer.

KT: *Both works are indifferent to each other and these two activities are, in different ways, very necessary to you. Will you continue to work in this style, and not put more weight on filmmaking in the future?*

T: Obviously, it's much easier, in terms of finance, to write than to make a film. As an independent, you are always struggling for access to the means of production, and the time it takes to raise funds is three or four times more than the time it takes to make the film. So even though I love both activities as much as each other, filmmaking is always special, and whenever it is possible, I give priority to film, because the opportunity is rare and difficult to get. But, so far I haven't even had to make that choice because fundraising takes so much time that I can only write in between the completion of each film.

KT: *So it's the situation . . . I've thought that there must be some reason that you are working on both fields and that there is something in common in both. Perhaps music might connect these two things. In translating your books I felt that there is some rhythm in your writing. My impression is that your books are strongly theoretical, not in the western sense of the term, but in the sense that your discussion is very persistent and not easily satisfied with some given "postmodern" (in a negative sense) framework prevailing in today's academicism. It is rhythm that seems to make your persistent theoretical discussions sound like poetry and your works different from those of great thinkers and writers like Derrida, Barthes or Foucault. In your films you often use the rhythm of percussion and beside this, your narration itself includes subtle rhythms. Could you speak about your attitude toward music or its relationship with your writing and filmmaking?*

T: Earlier you mentioned the influence of French thinkers and certainly that was a part of my background, but since I was interested in many other writers as well, including those from Africa and Japan, I would like to link this to the question you raise. One way to look at my work is to see how it resonates with Japanese visual and performing arts, for example. I've discussed how in working with words, you have to remain alert to the double empowering and enslaving potential of language; and for this, it is necessary to show the mechanisms of language, the way it functions and operates in the creative process. Rhythm should then be taken in the larger sense of the term, in its aesthetic, social and spiritual dimension.

Chinese artists, for example, did not talk about aesthetic when they elaborated on the precise criteria of traditional painting. But the main principles they expand on all revolve around the notion of *chi*, translated as the spirit and breath that a work arouses.

For me, *chi* is rhythm in both its micro- and macrocosmic scope. (KT: *Maybe we Japanese call it "ki", a stream of breeze or something that gets out of our body and something that comes into our body.*) Between wind and breath, there is the rhythm that regulates nature and the rhythm that animates your body. Nothing is difficult to understand here: when someone is sick or disturbed, the person breathes very differently than when she or he is fully alive, alert, and peaceful. Just as you listen to someone breathing, you listen to the way someone speaks, and similarly, to the way a film either subtly, powerfully, and playfully works with rhythm or remains unaware and hence lacks rhythm.

Rhythm is the door between mind and body. This should be nothing new for Japanese viewers and readers because in Japanese arts there are many examples of works that go beyond the message, the story, or the description of a reality to enter into the very gestures of creation. Films like Hirokazu Koreeda's *Maborosi*, which tells me so much about light and lighting, or Masahiro Shinoda's *Double Suicide*, made earlier in 1969, are just two among many other possible examples. When I first saw *Double Suicide* I was struck by the reflexive space it creates between theatre, film and calligraphy. Beside the fact that it incorporates the practices of Bunraku, the film's emotive vocal gestures, its explicit changes of settings, and its use of the men covered in black as a device to pull the viewer in and out of the screen story as well as to punctuate the course of events are both funny and captivating. The visible role given to these stage assistants or to the gesture of labor has been adapted in Ariane Mnouchkine's Shakespearean plays and fascinated Sergei Eisenstein, whose films also took inspiration from Toshusai Sharaku's actor prints. It is well known how much Japanese and Chinese theater inspired Bertolt Brecht's revolutionary theater and its alienating effects, just as Balinese dance vivified Antonin Artaud's Theater of Cruelty. This is not to mention the wave of artists in the West on whom Zen Buddhism and Yoga meditation have made a radical impact. The East's contribution to Western avant-garde in the arts, the humanities, and social sciences has been far-reaching. That's why I'm saying that presenting the gestures of creation while creating or while telling the story and the message is nothing new to a Japanese audience, even though the way we materialize this on film, of course, is unique to each artist.

Showing the stage assistants on screen or showing the creative process is not a mere question of making visible what is invisible. The fact that these men have covered their faces and bodies in black means that when we see them on stage or on screen, we see veiled black forms or the so-called color of invisibility itself. Such a break with the dichotomy between the visible and the invisible is what I have developed on my own and in many different ways in my written and film work. The process is not naively that of making visible what has been kept invisible (as in the case of works that seek to construct a positive image of a marginalized group), but that of working with what remains invisible in what presents itself visibly to us, or with the visible representation of invisibility itself. To bring out playfully the complexity of the presence of an absence and the absence of a presence is to work intimately with rhythm. In the movements created with what we can see and what we cannot see, rhythm plays a major role.

KT: *In your film, rhythm helps the audience focus upon your story (not a plot); the story or the process of your narration. Without it, it might go into pieces, I don't know, but this is working instinctively in your writing or in your films, I think.*

T: That's why when people focus too much on ideas and meanings and get frustrated because they can't take hold of a stable ground, they are missing that very instinctive working, or that whole dimension of the film experience, which does not require them to "understand" anything. With scrutiny, what thing, event or person does not ultimately fall to pieces and return to dust?

KT: *Now, can I ask you about sexuality issues? The subtitle of* Woman, Native, Other *is "Writing Postcoloniality and Feminism." In your films it seems you treat contemporary women's problematics, directly or indirectly, in postcolonial terms. I think your treatment of women focuses upon mainly gender issues, not upon sexuality, although the issues of gender and sexuality cannot be discussed separately and we should discuss how interrelated they are to each other. There are several very erotic scenes in your film* Reassemblage, *for instance the silhouette of a woman's bare breast. Thinkers such as Roland Barthes, Foucault, Deleuze and Guattari and writers such as Cixous and Duras, whom you mentioned in your books, speak directly about sexuality or they are in a very delicate position in terms of sexuality, as in the case of Roland Barthes or Michel Foucault. What do you think about sexuality and are you planning to treat sexuality as a main topic of your future work? For, the issue in which this interview will appear features "gender/sexuality."*

T: Even though there are many things my work touch on, these can be touched on indirectly, without necessarily my focusing on them. It's impossible to be exhaustive in any case; what I prefer is to provide tools workable across struggles. The example you gave of *Reassemblage*, with the shots of women's breasts clearly acknowledging the camera's look, have provoked highly controversial responses from viewers, both men and women. Again, these responses tell me how we have come to look at women's breasts—sexually, most of the time, and hence as something forbidden, if not pornographic, which we should feel embarrassed looking at, but which TV documentaries never fail to show surreptitiously as part of the exoticism of remote cultures. The way they are conventionally shot and covertly shown also tells me of people's general reluctance to recognize, among other things, their own desire to look at women's bare breasts.

By using close-ups in a wide range of framings, by not avoiding the fact that these breasts engage me visually, and in some instances, by contemplating rather than merely looking at them, I was, in fact, dealing personally and collectively with the question of sexuality. On one hand, women's breasts can be so many things aside from being a sexual attribute—the film shows a range of functions and of possibilities of reading images of women's breasts: included are tiny girls' breasts, rounded teenagers' breasts, mature mothers' breasts as well as withering grandmothers' breasts. How can one limit these to a sexual function or reduce them to a modern form of sexuality that equates women with nature and animality? In fact, some of the best readings I've had of these sequences of bare-breast women came from women viewers—both lesbians and heterosexuals.

On the other hand, you can say with Foucault and with the issues raised here that although some of us may have carried sexuality to its limits, we have not really liberated it, as long as we remain attached to mere positivism in representation. You should be able to "affirm non-positively" sexuality, which means that desire, eroticism, and sexuality are not merely to be found in the content of an image or a statement, but

also in the way a film is made, a rhythm is created, a music is composed and a text is written. It is in this dimension, in the tones, gestures, and processes of creativity that I address sexuality indirectly in my works, even though the forms of sexuality raised by *Reassemblage* or by *A Tale of Love* (which also carries scenes overtly addressing voyeurism and sexuality), for example, are definitely more recognizable.

KT: *Lastly, I'd like to ask you about your plan to shoot in Japan. What kind of matters interest you in Japan? What kind of film do you want to make about Japan? Will you treat sexuality or spirituality, or both as your theme?*

T: I am quite unable to talk about my future project simply because its ideas are growing and shifting with different encounters, and what I think at this minute may have already changed an hour or a day later. I can only speak in very broad terms. I've been traveling and shooting video while doing research for my next film. As with many foreign visitors who have been beneficiaries of the clearly defined relation between host and guest in Japan, I am drawn to what can be called the sense of life as performative art—the role that each member plays with ingenuity and commitment in a social situation, or the active function of each element in a cultural context.

Shooting in Japan also means dealing with the rituals of life that are both conservative forces of social cohesion and dynamic structures that contribute to creating a field of relations in which new, challenging interactions between past and present are possible. Rituals dwell, for example, in people's daily gestures; in the graphic and mobile quality of Japanese traditional architecture; in the precise organization of the railroad system; in the choreography of a festival event; in the artistry of a Kyoto meal; or in the rhythmic display of colors in street shops.

It seems important that the mythology of Japan's cultural insularity be challenged, especially in these times when Japan as a global economic power finds itself struggling at an uneasy moment in its history, having to re-orient itself in its attempts at turning toward Asia without turning its back on the West. I don't know yet what form sexuality will take in my next projects. To link with the question of rhythm which we discussed earlier, you can say that as a door between body and mind, a rhythm specific to a ritual or, let's say, to the graphic architecture of a temple, can also open a passage between sexuality and spirituality—a site that becomes at once more familiar and strange to me as I work more intensely on it.

KT: *Without any explicit scheme or plan in your mind in advance, you are making a vision, gathering and editing various encounters you have in the process of making films. This question might be inadequate since it is a kind of categorization, but will your new film about Japan be a narrative or a documentary film?*

T: I have a video project and a film project in mind. The video can be located more as a documentary, while the film is a fiction project. As I've specified in *Reassemblage* and with the films I've made, I don't make films *about* any specific culture, but more creatively and more challengingly, I can make a film that gets its inspiration from the inner structures and gestures of the culture.

IS FEMINISM DEAD?

with Fukuko Kobayashi

First published as "Deep Vibrancy of Silence: Interview with Trinh T. Minh-ha," in *The Rising Generation* (Tokyo, Japan), Vol. 146, No.2, May 2000.

Kobayashi: *You have published two books of criticism in Japan,* Woman, Native, Other *and* When the Moon Waxes Red, *both of which cut across diverse disciplines, such as feminist criticism, women's studies, film studies, and cultural studies. You have also directed five internationally acclaimed films, including* Reassemblage *and* Surname Viet, Given Name Nam. *These two films question the representation of Third World women. All of them blur the conventional boundaries of fact and fiction, theory and art, and poetry and politics. But precisely because of this tendency of yours to resist easy categorization, you initially had great difficulty in having your works published or screened. Would you tell us something about that?*

Trinh: To take into consideration this journal's readership, I should probably start with some of the difficulties I initially encountered within the Asian American community. A well-known filmmaker in this community told me, for example, that my film *Reassemblage* was not really Asian because of its colors. When I asked her what colors it should have in order to look or to be Asian, she affirmed that these were usually muted, whereas the colors of the films I shot in Africa were rather bold, lively and multifarious; for her, such an assertive abundance of colors was not very Asian. This is a nice, indirect way of tackling the problem. Most discontented viewers would simply say: "Why go and shoot films in Africa? Why not film our community and focus on what is relevant to Asians?"

We keep on returning to this notion of authenticity that is dealt with critically in my films and books. And I can't complain because even the hostile reactions to these works are part of their challenge. Related to this issue and perhaps of wider scope is another discussion, often resulting from the multilayered and expansive nature of my work, on how "Asianness" is produced. One of the concerns films like mine used to raise among film festival programers has to do, for example, with whether the selection of a film for an Asian American event should be made based on its subject matter (here, on Asian subjects) or on the maker's ethnicity (the fact that the filmmaker is of Asian descent). It's the whole question of what is Asian and who qualifies as Asian American.

And within the Asian American community there's also, to put it more constructively, a differential politics toward the first, second and third generations of Asian Americans. Old timers see newcomers like myself as belonging more to the Asian than to the Asian American world; partly because the formation of a Vietnamese Diaspora in the U.S is relatively recent; but mainly, I would say, because there's a difference of mentality between the first and third generations of immigrants in relation to assimilation and resistance. Similar foreclosures may also be found in the reception of the books you mentioned.

The educational system is still widely invested in maintaining boundaries between disciplines. This is noticeable in the way specialized knowledge continues to dominate. Asian American, African American, Chicano and Native American studies are, for example, often conceived of as totally separate programs in institutionalized networks. The margins remain, as expected, fragmented and disconnected despite the logistics that pull them together. It used to be that people in one area of study were not aware of the struggles of peoples in the other areas. But today—and I hope this is what my work has contributed to—with crossovers in postcolonial, ethnic and other studies, younger generations of students seem much more eager to learn across struggles and less stuck within the confines of established territories. So that which was at the base of the difficulties and constant obstacles I encountered when my books were sent out to seek publication is now being made a subject of study in progressive venues. Although the system is far from being *inter-*, *post-* and *trans-*disciplinary, hopefully things are changing in this direction.

K: *I'm very glad you raised this issue, because I was about to tell you what happened when I first came across your work. It was when your early films were screened in the Asian American Film Festival held in Shibuya by Image Forum in 1993. At that time I had just begun to be interested in so-called Asian American literature, so I happily went there hoping to learn something about Asian American culture. What I came across was your* Reassemblage, *a film dealing with women in Senegal. And so you can imagine how it intrigued me. I then read in Image Forum's journal that Darryl Chin, who was the organizer of that festival, wished that they could have included more films like yours, whose subject matter was not confined to Asian American themes, but they couldn't do so because it was the so-called Asian American film festival. But what I'd like to ask you is do you consider yourself Asian American? or in a different manner? Because I feel you don't talk of yourself that way.*

T: For me, all of these labels are, at worst, confining. But depending on the context, a label can be at times a constructive tool, especially when it is used convivially as a device to gather works together in order to help with their circulation. This was the case with *Reassemblage* when you first saw it. Thanks to the insistence of Tomiyama Katsue and her staff at Image Forum, I was able to accompany the film. At the time, my being selected (with Gregg Araki) as a representative Asian American did come as a surprise for both sides: for the American co-sponsors of the festival, who had other

Asian American filmmakers in mind, and for the audiences across Japan who came to the event not expecting to hear any views critical of America. Even for an event like that, which took place, not in the U.S nor in Vietnam, but on a third ground, I am still slightly out of place. So a label used strategically can constitute a means to draw attention to what tends to be neglected and to give exposure to works that rarely get to be seen. That's when labels are at their best. But I think most of the time they invite conformity and, in the long run or in a wider scope, they prove to be extremely confining.

K: *Would you be offended then if you were called Vietnamese American?*

T: It depends on who calls you that and why. I would say that sometimes the context and the intention are quite harmless. For example, if someone in Asia introduces me as such, I would say it's because the person wants to emphasize the fact that I'm part of Asia. As it's well-intended, I don't have any problem with that.

K: *Good. Because sometimes I have to introduce you that way although I try not to, if possible.*

T: But imagine it being used in another context—as a way to exclude you, for example. That your work can only be seen when it is classified in a specific category also means that it has no place in other general, more inclusive categories. The category determines the way the work is circulated and discussed; it becomes easily confined to predefined, pre-assigned slots. This is when, for me, labels become asphyxiating. What often happens is that throughout the years, because of who you are (biologically) rather than what you do or where you go (socially and politically), you are expected to conform to limited areas of activity. Once people perceive you as so and so, they constantly ask you to do more of the same, to speak as a postcolonial or a Third World woman, for example, or else to speak on Asian Americans, on ethnic identity, on your own culture. Whether intentional or not, it's a way to contain and control the scope of our activities.

K: *Since your works are all very provocative, they have often caused violent reactions. Perhaps one of the things that exasperate some of your audiences is your use of so-called stereotypes. You don't completely denounce them, but rather try to use them for your own purposes, like when you compare women to the moon in* When the Moon Waxes Red. *Some people might say you should not talk that way. Could you state how you use stereotypes or rather your attitude toward them?*

T: First of all, I rarely use the term stereotype myself. Ideology criticism has taught us to denounce reductive forms of representation, but it has serious limits. Most of the time this kind of criticism leads to a dead end because it tends to block the very space of criticism with angry accusations in which "stereotype" is merely equated with lies and falseness: You're repeating stereotypes of Us! Okay, but each one of us can accuse the other of falling prey to stereotypes when it comes to endorsing Our authority on the matter. So where does this lead us? Nowhere. We simply throw stones at one another and stop at charges such as: "You are making a stereotype out of this and that." But if someone asks, "What makes it a stereotype? How does it function?" or "You are making a stereotype with this image and investing into this stereotype, why?" and further inquires about how you work with that stereotype, then it starts becoming interesting. What happens then to the stereotype? Assuming that we agree on why it is a stereotype, it can, as a deliberate device, predetermine the way you see things or accordingly serve to change it. You start somewhere in order to go somewhere else, and something ready-made gets subtly unmade. With humour and irony, for example, stereotypes can be used both to expose and to undermine stereotypes themselves.

For me, rather than talking about stereotypes, I would say that our languages and images are full of clichés; that in our desire to grasp things quickly we tend to fix things and to arrest forms rather than follow them in their shifting realities. So when someone says you can't talk of the moon and women together, all this person does is censor you. The assumption that there is an identification between the two is also highly reductive, for this is not how the moon nor how women are spoken of in *When the Moon Waxes Red*. What is called the Moon is treated both literally—with its cycles and shifting forms—and figuratively. And what is involved is not one but a multiplicity of metaphors, or an ongoing process of metamorphosing. The book does not begin with women. It begins with time, motion and stillness; with the image of a white light in an empty room, followed by one of yellow sprouts, which hints at a totally different dimension of the Moon, or if you prefer, of awareness. As we move on, there is a play on the Old Moon and the New Moon in references to Chinese mythology and Western science. Then comes the political dimension of the Moon as related to the Cultural Revolution in China, which I recall with humor while working critically on its association with women. It was clear in the book that as long as you only speak about the Moon as being dependent on the Sun, then woman is not "Woman" (with capital W) and she would refuse to be confined to the Moon. The "moon" is a name and so is "woman." In using names to decompose names, you can see how profoundly ingrained our prejudices remain in our language.

K: *Part of* When the Moon Waxes Red *was written while you were writing* Woman, Native, Other. *When I first read* When the Moon Waxes Red, *I was struck that in that book you seemed to be moving in a new direction. In chapters 9, 11, 13 and the preface titled "Yellow Sprouts," you make frequent references to such traditional Eastern art forms as Chinese poetry, painting, calligraphy, haiku, and so on. It was all the more striking because in your first book, you seemed to be far more concerned with African culture. Could you explain this shift in your second book, if you agree to call it a "shift?"*

T: When I wrote *Woman, Native, Other*, I had just moved back from Senegal. Living there for three years was a catalyzing experience, for it was in Africa, not in Asia, that I actually developed a sense of Third World solidarity. The book was very much suffused with that reality of Africa and how it changed my experience of what one might call the "Asian" or the "American" reality. So the shift you see is related to circumstances: the encounter with African culture allowed me, in *When the Moon Waxes Red*, to come back to Asian culture in a different way; there is, so to say, no naive return to the roots.

K: *I personally found the style of* When the Moon Waxes Red *fascinating; that is one reason why I decided to translate it. I call it haiku-like because it has a lot of what you might call "ellipses" or "silences." Would you comment on the use of silence in your work?*

T: I would relate the use of ellipses, as you mention, and of silence to my musical background. We tend to grasp music as sound and focus on sound formation, but with composers like Toru Takemitsu or John Cage, for example, we return to the simple fact that silence is where we all head for in our life journey. Silence is not accidental, it is fundamental. We spend our whole lifetime either avoiding it or widening our ability to listen to it. Those who are aware of its deep vibrancy also turn their whole attention to the single sound, to intervals, relationships, movements and dynamics—in other words to both the undoing and the doing of silence as the basic utterance of sound. The East has been saying this for millennia, but it took the work of someone like Cage for such a return to the basic form of music to become an influence in the West—something that has been revolutionizing not only music, but all of the arts in the modern world.

One of Rauschenberg's pieces of art offers a famous example, in which what you see as a "painting" is a mere white canvas. People would go to an exhibition just to look at a blank canvas on which they might see, according to the time of day, their own or others' temporal shadows. The same thing can be said of silence in the social and political context of women or of marginalized groups. I can't emphasize enough the importance of a third ground in all processes of transformation. As I've suggested, my encounter with African culture makes a huge difference in the way I live the Asian American reality. Without it, a tendency, for example, to simply accept the kind of silence that I grew up with in an Asian culture would be almost unavoidable. Asian cultures know the value of silence, which is in itself a language. But when it becomes so much part of our identity, it can turn out to be a place of deep confinement and repression. We recognize this in every aspect of social life, including in the daily family context where women, not supposed to voice their thoughts in broad daylight, have been silenced even before they start exploring a language. In such a context, the question of silence is extremely difficult to deal with.

The task of writing with silence is delicate. If you deal with only the seen and the heard, then you come up with a text in which words are written only for the sake of ideas and feelings; that is, primarily in a state of servility—to illustrate concepts, messages and emotions. Whereas if "sounds are sounds and people are people," as Cage put it, or if language only communicates with language, as Walter Benjamin remarked, then a third movement is involved in which writing neither falls prey to self-expression nor does it serve as a mere instrument for thoughts. To go more directly to my own text, I would say silence has to do with rhythm—that is, with language as intervals and relationships. Most of the time when I write, I conceive a sentence not only in terms of what it says for the sake of having something to say, but also in terms of when, where, and how it says it—and unsays it. As with a "musical" phrase, such a sentence has a movement and a life of its own. You can cut a sentence off abruptly but you have to be very sharp and incisive in the way you cut it. For the sake of music as well as of sense and grammar, you can't just cut it anywhere. You may first feel about and, trusting your creative impulse, you work on it to see where it leads you. You devise your own rules as you advance, you open up the field of possibilities in meaning and, as a result, you contribute to the emergence of a "voice"—your own.

K: *To change the subject: at present there seems to exist a great deal of interest in autobiographical writing among marginalized groups of writers in the U.S., particularly among the so-called "women of color" writers, Gloria Anzaldua, Maxine Hong Kingston among them. And it is largely in order to rename themselves in the face of the ever-pernicious drive for name-calling or stereotyping on the part of mainstream media that they are so keen on writing autobiographies. But you seem to maintain a somewhat ambivalent relationship to autobiography. While both your critical and film works are often said to be unusually self-revealing—your documentaries, for example, are called "personal documentaries"—you've hardly done any straightforward autobiographical writing. Why such a reservation?*

T: Yes, that's very nicely put since it all depends on how we define autobiography. If autobiography is only about the personal or only about yourself as an individual, then I have little affinity with it. The same applies to the work of criticism I have done. In the chapter of *Woman, Native, Other* on anthropology, for example, I buried the white male anthropologists' names in the footnotes. I was not interested in criticizing individuals, I was much more concerned with the representative space they occupy, or with the conditions and contexts that allow their authority to go unchallenged. To expose one's critical relation to some of the West's most confident discourses caught in the circuit of colonialist values is ultimately to face one's own dominant "I." So although social values exert their power through specific individuals, what I challenge is an institutionalized tradition of articulating and valorizing, not the individuals per se.

The same thing applies when it comes to autobiography. What is the self? To reduce it to the personality of an individual is to indulge in the die-hard "myth of the artist" or "myth of the writer." It is one thing to learn how to politicize the personal, as in the case of women and people of color. It is another thing to cater to the West's ideology of individualism and its mania for uncovering the private lives of famed individuals. The focus on the personal story of success or failure makes that story politically harmless by confining it to the partial realm of an individual's case. Writing as a vocation is only possible when the personal is where one immediately encounters society without losing the individual. So if autobiography involves primarily the social self, then you'll find plenty of autobiographical elements in my work. You can recognize me or locate me everywhere in my film, in every framing, every cut, every camera gesture. What I offer the viewer is not an impersonal look at an event or a culture. Look, meaning, voice, and rhythm are here precisely situated, but as you can see, this is not a question of showing an individual point of view. It's more a question of sharing the tools of creativity, of expanding the cinematic language, and of positioning oneself in relation to the specific event portrayed. These are far more important in any integral "autobiographical" approach. And, as you've mentioned, it is significant that "writers of color" and "writers from the Third World" should be the ones to make extensive use of this genre and to hybridize it. Terms like "autoethnography" have been used to refer to Zora Neale Hurston's work and Audre Lorde called her own attempt (in *Zami*) a "bio-mythography."

This ongoing questioning of a normalized, reductive form of autobiography is here a necessity.

K: *There is also a tendency for so-called "women writers from the Third World" to become used for commercial purposes, so they tend to be put in a neat category. There is this question nowadays also, I think.*

T: Oh, very much, unfortunately. I think Toni Morrison wrote very nicely about this when she said that a large part of the African American literary heritage has been the autobiography. It is mainly through this genre that marginalized writers' voices are consumed. But the difficulty, as American slaves' self-narratives exemplify, is to tell a story that is at the same time personal and representative of the race, and to work "objectively" (so as not to offend the white readership) within a genre that can be easily dismissed as "biased" or "partial" since, unlike works of theory, autobiographies only feature a harmless individual case. In using their own lives to expose the horrors of slavery, these writers were always walking the fine line of appealing to the high-mindedness of White readership while remaining true to the collective suffering of their people or to the potential Black reader.

Here, as you can see, the notion of autobiography has already been twisted, because in the case of colonized and oppressed people, they are always socialized to see more than one point of view—that of the dominant and that of the dominated—and this shows in the careful tone and selection of the material that forms the narrative. The same applies for women. On the one hand, it's so much easier to appeal to a wider audience by publishing autobiographical writings—this is what a potential literary agent keeps on reminding me, "We would love to read about your life" she says. But on the other hand, we have to resist these pre-assigned slots to which women and marginalized groups are expected to confine themselves.

K: *Yes, and they tend to make rather reductive readings of your work based upon the autobiographical facts, especially when the writers are women, or from the Third World. In* Woman, Native, Other, *you quoted* Dictee *by Theresa Hak Kyung Cha, a woman writer of Korean descent who died prematurely. You must be among the very few who noticed the significance of her text at such an early stage. The book was long ignored due to its extremely complex, multilayered nature. Were you personally acquainted with Cha in her lifetime? I'm curious because you two seem to have so much in common.*

T: Well, it's very nice that you mention her book because it's one of the few works that I still love today. In fact, there are many works that I love but cannot read any more. This is the case, for example, with works by Helene Cixous or even John Cage. I read them too much and then they become too familiar, too recognizable. But *Dictee* is an exception: I teach it every year in one of my classes, and every time I come back to it, I rediscover it. This ability to speak anew each time is perhaps due to something we discussed earlier in relation to my books—the fact that her writing is also very elliptical. She was fearless in assuming her multifragmented, stuttering linguistic identity, shifting abruptly from French to English to Korean. In *Dictee* there are layers of conversation between the blank space and the printed space, and between the photograph and the written word. As she was also a film and video artist, her text is at times more like a film script that tells us what to see by following the camera's point of view in the scenes she composed. The space of memory and autobiography is where the historical, the personal, the sexual, the linguistic, the musical and the filmic meet so intricately.

Looking at her mother and her suffering is looking at the condition of a whole generation of Asian women in their relation to silence and language. But a very nice touch for me and certainly one that my students often seem to have a problem with, is that, in dealing with the autobiographical, Cha never claims the insider's position of truth nor makes use of the internal psychological voice. She looks at her mother from the outside, the way a camera looks at its subject. She looks through and as a camera (objectively, almost as an outsider) at her mother, or at her own self, and she describes the scene of suffering only through what the eye of the camera can catch. Such a formal device heightens the emotion rather than diminishes it. The distance and the understatement contribute to an intensification of the emotion. This is what I truly love; the fact that she's able to find other ways of speaking about the self, about insiderness, without simply resorting to the authority of the insider's voice.

K: *Well, I am so glad that you raised this issue of emotion because I was happy to discover in* Framer Framed, *an anthology of your scripts and interviews, that you mentioned that the motivation for* Reassemblage *was not resistance to anthropology but your love for the subject of inquiry, namely women in Senegal.*

T: And their culture.

K: *Yes, their culture, too. And in the same book, you said that what you see in* Surname Viet Given Name Nam *is your own commitment to the feminist struggle. Since many people prefer just to talk about the deconstructive side of those films—particularly in Japan—I'm happy that you mentioned this. For I myself reacted rather emotionally to those films, not just intellectually. So would you please comment on this aspect?*

T: Yes, it's a strange thing, these contradictory reactions to my film. I notice them all the time. And you are certainly not the only one to feel this way. I have met women who were very, very strongly emotionally . . . how should I put it . . . not only moved, but for whom the experience of the film changed their lives. Young American women came to me, bursting into tears saying they had cried their heart out, unable to believe someone could have made such a film. It was the first time they had seen something like that, they said, and they spoke ecstatically about its enabling effects on their realities. I've also met mature women in Europe who told me how much of themselves and their lives they saw unfolding on the screen as they followed the stories of the women featured.

The realm of emotion is one that we are not willing to acknowledge, especially in intellectual and academic milieus. How a film affects your body, how a work affects your senses and your self is something that I rarely encounter in analyses of my work. The only critics who dare to do that are apparently those who are themselves dealing with many levels of emotion in their own works. Someone like Alberto Moravia, the late Italian novelist. When Moravia wrote about *Reassemblage*, he immediately said how that film affected him physically. I loved that, I love to hear of the direct experience of the viewer's body, the sensual experience that people feel before they make

sense of anything happening. What he gave was more than insight; it was a way of loving, a truth of the creative moment that bound the viewer to the maker. And it's not as if emotions are lacking or absent in audiences' reponses. They are very present and often viscerally expressed. Many viewers have come to me and told me about this kind of reaction. It's just that in the area of criticism, very few people who write acknowledge that part of a response to film; they fear that it may appear too "personal" or "subjective" because they don't know how to deal with emotion otherwise than psychologically. We need to devise new tools. The experience of film is not merely about story line, message or political engagement.

K: *Talking about your recent film work, I am most interested in the latest development shown in* A Tale of Love. *It is your first narrative film; though you've always tended to blur the distinction between fact and fiction. Could you tell me why you chose this form of film?*

T: It's not the usual narrative film because it doesn't have a central story. It has a semblance of a story in the beginning, but as the film moves on, it becomes clear for most viewers that it is a no-story film because the story does not develop; it does not wrap up; it just unfolds as a space of interrelations and interstories. So *A Tale of Love* offers no straight narrative even though, as your question implies, unlike with my previous films, it is composed of carefully scripted material. But whatever the genre one works with, the important thing is to push the boundaries of well-established categories.

There's always this tendency to separate for better control and to reduce life to a storyline. History is reduced to a line, so are the individual stories that form its fabric. The density and thickness of events, the spatial, the temporal, the historical, and the social are often reduced to a question of numbers and chronology. Whereas in "documenting," for example, what seems necessary to me is precisely to address the impossibility of packaging information in linear fashion and to bring out the complexities of these encounters between realities, between cultures or between subjectivities. This is why with the earlier films I've made, I haven't started with a preconceived idea; in other words, I don't shoot in order "to cover a story" as media people put it; I don't use film merely to inform or to convey a political message. When I'm on the site, I remain alert to everything that happens during the process of shooting and to how reality speaks to me in these moments of encounter. A putting into practice of freedom like this has its own rules and it is very different from the one I developed with *A Tale of Love.* Since I wrote a script for this film, there was a blueprint for everything right down to the smallest detail. But unlike in mainstream films, where details are scripted only so as to serve the plot and to conform to the central story line, in my film the precise detailing serves no central purpose. Although the details are carefully thought out, they have, so to say, their own stories to tell. As with the complexity of life, we see people in the street walking resolutely in different directions, but we don't know exactly where, why and to what purpose. Yet the multiplicity of things does not appear pointless to us, as we know we each organize our life quite minutely and we all have our reasons and motives for going where we go. So despite the difference between these two ways of putting into practice of freedom, there's a vein of resistance that runs similarly through my films, whether these are called documentary or fiction.

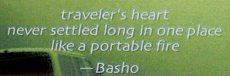

traveler's heart
never settled long in one place
like a portable fire
— Basho

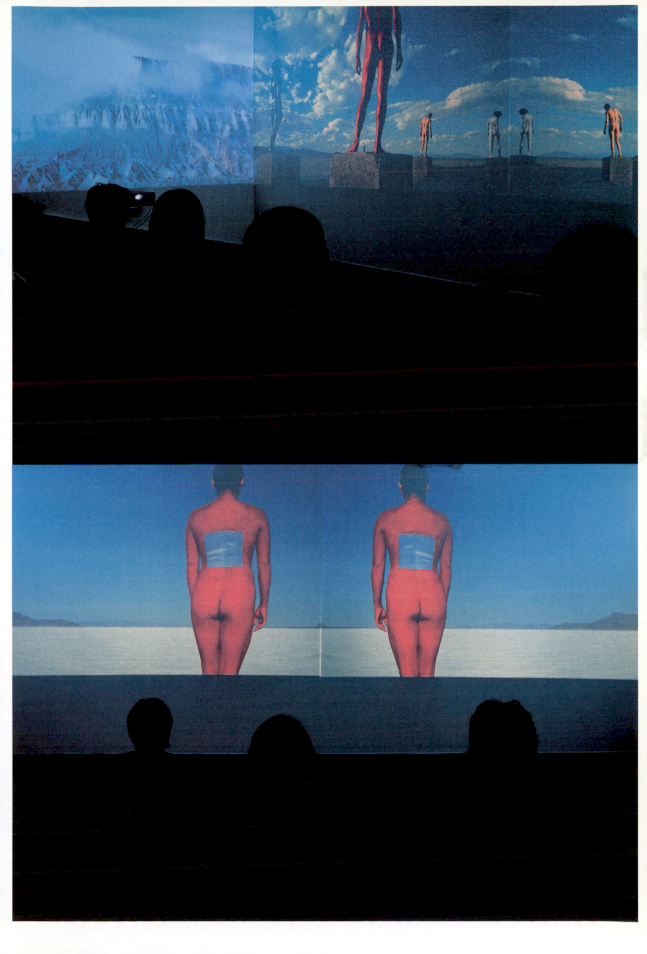

"Which Side?" Photo and body art by Jean-Paul Bourdier in *The Desert Is Watching*.

K: *Perhaps partly because you shot* A Tale of Love *with a 35-mm camera for the first time, I felt each scene of it was strikingly beautiful. Some people who saw the excerpts of your third film,* Shoot for the Contents, *at Ochanomizu Gender Studies Center, seemed to have been quite impressed with the beauty of it—even disturbed by it—because they felt your depiction of China appeared too beautiful. But I feel there is a fixed idea that anything truly experimental should not be too beautiful—the alternative feminist cinema of the '80s, for example. How do you explain your use of beauty in your work?*

T: Yes, it's quite a pertinent question in relation to the world of progressive, experimental, or political filmmakers. As the saying goes, "The bigger the grain (of the image), the better the politics." The more an image is hard on the eyes, shaky or unrefined, the more experimental or political it is thought to be. There is, of course, some truth here, but this straight reversal stance has become such a cliché today, and anti-aestheticism has proven to be a style like any other. A stance and a style that often serve to hide the very shortcomings of a large number of productions—the fact that they remain unaware of their "framings," or of their own politics as cinema and as representation. What is perpetuated when a work dwells on the convenient opposition between form and content is the state of servility in which the camera and the cinematic medium are kept—to conform to a story line or to a message, for example. There are many uses to which you can put a film, and it's fine to resort to what one can call its activist or journalistic use. But then this limited use should not become a way to hide other issues.

Politics and experiments may be at odds with beauty as a value and as a narrow bourgeois preoccupation, but the political and the experimental themselves cannot be taken for granted as they have also become fixed, consumable categories today. Why attack beauty only, when "documentary," "political," "narrative," "avant-garde," "experimental" or "alternative" as applied to cinema have become more indicative of a genre than of a field of unexpected, subversive activities. That's why when I go to film festivals as a juror, I'm always disturbed by the fact that experimental works look so much alike; this is because of the existence of a repertoire of avant-garde techniques in filmmaking. It is not surprising then, as your question pertinently implies, that the explicit beauty of *A Tale of Love* did intermittently cause hostility among members of experimental film audiences (just as *Shoot for the Contents* did among some documentary film consumers), who in any case had not been supportive of my film *Reassemblage* either, when it first came out. It took a lot of persistence for people to realize what is at stake in these films, for which they have no adequate tools to criticize.

It suffices to give a little attention to the way the components of cinema work in *A Tale of Love* to recognize that its beauty has a context. In other words, there's quite a difference to be made between a beauty encased in naturalized conventions and a beauty that is openly reflexive and performative. I have elaborated on the necessity in *A Tale* not to go after the "natural" look, but to deal with beauty in its artifices and its rituals—love on film as a ceremony and a cinegraphy. No realist locations, no naturalistic acting, no made-to-believe dialogues and characters; in brief, no psychological realism in the film; so the notion of beauty has to emerge from a different context. What is constructed through the art of artifices should artfully display its artificiality.

K: *One more thing about* A Tale of Love. *I'm interested in your choice of subject matter. You explore in it the theme of love from multiple angles. For quite a while it has been considered that romance or the ideology of love is the enemy of women, perpetuating male domination over women, and feminists somehow seem to have avoided prying into this matter. But recently, there seems to be a new revival of interest in this theme. Is your choice of subject matter somewhat consonant with this revival of interest in love?*

T: I don't think it is consonant in any intentional or conscious way. I was more concerned with the whole history of cinema. We can say that the love story and its voyeurism run through the history of narrative cinema. What commercial cinema sells is the love story. It was with a critical view of this context that I focused on love as a challenge to the relationship between lover and beloved, maker and viewer, actor and spectator or in other words, between seeing and seen. As a character says in the film, "Every story of love is a story of voyeurism." For the attentive ear and eye, this is what makes the difference between the story of love and the love story—the latter being blind to the instance of its consumption. Of course, the film can also be viewed as a tribute to the second wave of feminists' writings on love, which I have mentioned elsewhere. In the '70s women theorists wrote critically on love and on what they saw as the pivot of women's sexploitation and self-victimization. Passion, emotion, intuition and sex appeal were all too readily attributed to the domain of women. These are what we face intimately in love, and we know we can't condemn or deny them without cutting off a whole part of ourselves and our lives. So a tribute means that we recognize what has been done, not that we abide by the same historical logic of criticism. From there, we can move on. Of course, by focusing on love—an all-too-familiar ground—I have exposed myself to all kinds of possible misunderstandings and clichéd interpretations. As with the question of beauty, it is necessary here to distinguish the active from the reactive.

K: *I'd like to ask you about the present state of feminism. In Japan, quite a few people seem to be of the opinion that feminism has lost its role, saying, for example, that we should talk of gender, of postfeminism instead. The simpler reversal strategy adopted by the earlier feminists, as you call it in* When the Moon Waxes Red, *should certainly be criticized, but I feel we should be rather careful in denouncing monolithically even the earlier form of feminism. It seems that some people do so simply because they want to feel trendy or fashionable, but I feel it is rather dangerous, for it can be part of what you call a "divide and conquer" attitude toward those who still try to support feminist causes. And what is so moving about* Surname Viet Given Name Nam *is your emphasis on the continuity from Vietnamese women living in the old Confucian regime to those living in a more democratic community in the States. Could you comment on this issue of continuity and discontinuity in feminism?*

T: Well, I myself don't hold on to the term feminism. When someone says, "It's dead," it's fine if it is dead. Only I need to know in what context the person is making such a statement. If it is in relation to trends and fashion, as you've mentioned, then it may not be worth my time to get engaged in the conversation, because, as with all liberation movements, you have people who just hop aboard and hop off when it's convenient for them. They are not the ones who carry on the struggle, who scrutinize their everyday practices, who work intimately and publicly at changing the conditions of women or at modifying the boundaries feminism. They are just "hoppers," that's all. But if someone says, "Feminism is dead" in a fully informed context of investigation, then I would ask, "What is dead?" Is the name dead? Is the label dead? Is the attitude dead? Is the moment of history dead? What exactly is dying? If the person elaborates on all these "dead things" in order to open up new ground, then I would support the effort and would walk with the person to explore this new ground. That would be totally fascinating.

So I don't hold on to this label of "feminism," but the strength, the force that motivates and underlies the feminist struggle is something that will never die. There are important nuances to emphasize here. Just because there's a backlash against feminism in the mainstream media does not mean that the feminist struggle has reached the end. On the contrary, I think that the situation all around the world today in terms of gender, nation and religion shows that the struggle is far from being over. The huge wave of conservative moves devised to police women's movements and appearance and to put them back into the recesses of the patriarchal home can be viewed as a reaction to the widespread action of feminism that has been making itself felt even in the remote parts of the world. The more coercive the ruling power is, the deeper the resistance of its subjects. The fact that this wave of oppression continues to rise is indicative of just how unstable these patriarchal regimes have come to be. It is when they feel most threatened and tighten their control that they show themselves to be a dying form. So for me, people who declare feminism has lost its role, depending on where they want to go with such a statement, maybe intentionally or unintentionally partaking in a dying form of oppression.

K: *So you can talk of postfeminism in the same manner. If it opens up to a new state, then you support this idea of postfeminism, namely the continuation and the new ground of feminism.*

T: Only if post feminism is used as a term to shift borders and to reopen anew the terrain of feminism. After all, postfeminism still has feminism in it; if people wish to do away entirely with feminism, they should use a totally different term. As it has been said in relation to postmodernism, "post" does not merely imply "after"; when placed in non-linear time, it also refers to the moments of beginnings, when the field of activity is at its most subversive. This being said, I don't think that's how the term is being used with the backlash in the media against feminism. The mainstream is very quick to appropriate feminism for its own ends and to appropriate it in such a way as to turn people who are less informed or the younger generation against feminism.

K: *May I ask you about your next film? Is it going to be more a so-called narrative than a documentary?*

T: I can't tell you this for sure because I actually have four projects. It all depends on where the funding comes from.

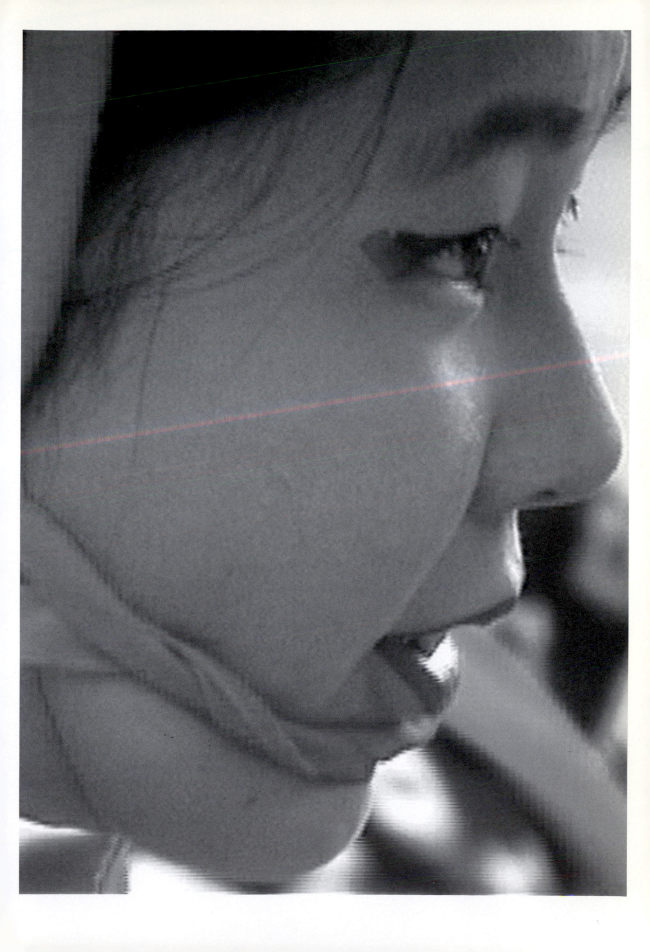

K: *Maybe this label will also disturb you. You said you are interested in making a film concerning spirituality: women and spirituality?*

T: Yes. But this is actually nothing new. You can see a spiritual dimension in all of my work. The subject is not something that can be discussed lightly, since spirituality has always resisted analytical thinking and the logic of consciousness. It's very difficult to speak about it, but I would simply say to start off with that I am not interested in institutionalized religion. What I am exploring is something more like spirituality in the margins. Resistance and spirituality: How do they go together? This is also very precarious ground to be walking on.

PART IV

INSTALLATIONS

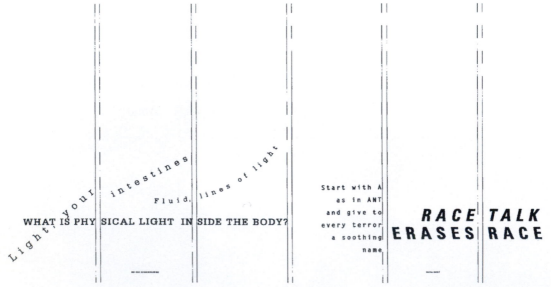

Light your intestines

Fluid, lines of light

WHAT IS PHYSICAL LIGHT INSIDE THE BODY?

Start with A
as in ANT
and give to
every terror
a soothing
name.

RACE TALK
ERASES RACE

NOTHING BUT WAYS

Installation

Trinh T. Minh-ha and Lynn Marie Kirby

Yerba Buena Center for the Arts, San Francisco,
June 4–August 15, 1999

Acetate film panels of different neutral densities; reflective vinyl lettering; tracking, pivoting Fresnel spot lights; motion sensors; contact microphones; amplifiers.

A large-scale, multimedia installation made as a tribute to the love of poetry, with a focus on the works of twelve women poets. An encounter of poetry on a cinematic canvas, the installation features the basic components of both media to offer a spatial experience of the screen/page. The event is also a walk into the body through word passages and a play on the activities of reflecting, projecting and vibrating that define the creative process of writing and reading.

Poets featured: Etel Adnan, Mei-mei Berssenbruge, Patricia Dienstfrey, Kathleen Frazer, Barbara Guest, Erica Hunt, June Jordan, Myung Mi Kim, Audre Lorde, Wendy Rose, Rena Rosenwasser, Alma Villanueva.

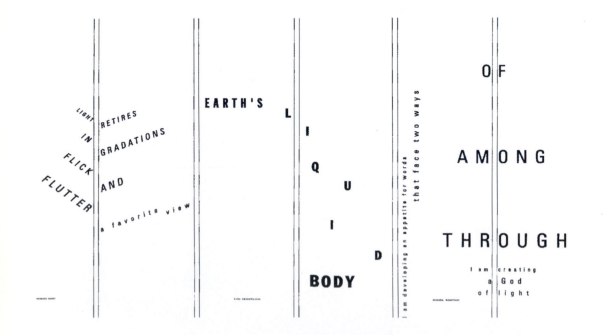

one full

estine

Black lily

luminescen

Flu

LIGHT IN   SIDE THE BODY?

LIGHT RETIRES   EARTH'S   L   OF

IN   GRADATIONS   I

FLICK   AND   Q   AMONG

FLUTTER   U

    a favorite view   I

                                 D   THROUGH

                                 BODY

NOTHING BUT WAYS

the encounter of poetry on a cinematic canvas
a many-and-one screen
with no spectacle to watch
simulation
film, eviscerated
its material components in-sight out
curves, curls
rolls winding into one another
ritual
in a gallery space

> *light*
> *in flick and flutter*
> *breaks through diffusing*
> *color*

what else in the journey
but
passages crossings
breatheways
less than wide, narrow, more than narrow
so it goes a mazelike
frame-per-frame
walk into words,
nearsighted
body strayed
to the heart of film
movement
twenty-four-frames-per-second
illusion

> *"because she's in a body, it makes decisions"*

chromatically it unfolds
under the hypnotic light of video
vibrations magnets
over the scrim
the imperceptible continual scanning
traces a digital image
pixels so close they lure your eye
womb voices and burrowed noises
suspending
that structural urge in spatial
-izing the visual a music you can touch

in the intracellular world of words images
that "quality of a light within"
that "skeleton architecture of our lives"
invites framing in darkness
"brings her running out of the hall,
bursting into the room, her arms open . . ."

> *did she say cinema or poetry?*
> *ah but this is not*
> *not a poem*

THE PAGE SCREEN CANVAS

with Lynn Marie Kirby and Victoria Alba

First published in *Artweek*, Issue 7/8, Vol. 30, July/August, 1999 with the following introductory review by Steve Jenkins, then editor-in-chief: *"To get lost in a book—in particular a work of fiction—is to enter a world imagined so completely by its author that, as readers, we're transported from our daily routines and familiar surroundings to some other time and place that resembles the crystal-clear landscape of a waking dream. If that sounds like sentimental rubbish in this era of meta-everything ironic distancing, in which the novel's ability to shape cultural discourse relies more on endorsement from Oprah than on any sense of intrinsic literary worthiness, I'll happily stick my neck out in declaring the ongoing pleasures of the text (with a nod to Roland Barthes). To read is to be seduced, to be read to is seduction, which at least partially explains the ongoing popularity of poetry slams among urbane hipsters in search of a reprieve from swing dancing.*

Let's not forget, however, that hand-stitched chapbooks of poetry sell in the hundreds, while tickets for The Phantom Menace *and* The Matrix *sell in the millions. The moral of this long story made very short is that we live in a predominantly visual culture in which film—the projected, moving image—has staked its claim as the century's undisputed form of high art and popular entertainment (although the twain rarely meet anymore). Mergings of books have resulted in an endless cycle of bodice-ripping adaptations, pointless remakes featuring the gruesome spectacle of Keanu Reeves reciting Shakespeare soliloquies, and the dreaded "based upon a true story" disclaimer. The pictures (as pioneering movie moguls called them) always have relied on fiction and poetry for content, yet rarely has cinema successfully conveyed the essence of books as fetishistic object, or as magic lanterns imprinting successions of words on our subconscious.*

Enter Lynn Kirby and Trinh T. Minh-ha, whose collaborative installation Nothing But Ways *is far more something than nothing, that something being an innovative environment in which the by-now-standard image/text*

symbiosis—a postmodern staple—is reconfigured as a floating world of larger-than-life words and big-screen fantasies in which our shadows play starring roles. Kirby and Trinh, both justly celebrated for their diverse media works, do a fine job of describing their project (see accompanying interview) so I'll add only some intentionally fragmentary impressions of their intimate epic that maps what they term "the encounter of poetry on a cinematic canvas." Swimming through the underwater blue of light and shadow—film's essential properties, making possible myriad narratives that Godard flippantly reduced to "a girl and a gun"—I felt like an extra in a big-budget extravaganza crowded with poet-know-it-scene-stealers. Strong, strange phrases—Patricia Diensfrey's "I am creating a God of light," June Jordan's "Black Lily/One full luminescent/in a handmade field of love," Audre Lorde's "I am a bleak heroism of words that refuse to be buried alive with the liars"—undulate on their acetate screens, as white noise emanates from dangling speakers.

It's like walking through the pages of a book, and while the gallery's bright-green "exit" sign points toward the end of the story, it's tempting to stay immersed forever. With polynarratives, shifting plot, phantom characters and deep blue mystery, Nothing But Ways *is what Cronenberg's* Existenz *should have been. Next time, Kirby and Trinh should adapt* Finnegan's Wake *as a musical comedy.*

Alba: *Could you tell me about Nothing But Ways?*

Trinh: To give you a context, the idea of making an installation came about two years ago. As a member of the advisory board of Kelsey Street Press—which publishes poetry or experimental writing by women—I wanted to contribute to the Press' effort to fundraise and to do outreach when, in order to secure a specific grant, they needed to come up with a project that would exceed the medium of the printed page. In view of the Press' series of collaboration between women poets and artists, I proposed a collaboration with Lynn [Kirby] who had been working with installations. The Press was very excited and started raising money for the installation. They also contacted Renny Pritikin at the Yerba Buena Center for the Arts, whose location and multicultural audience seemed best suited to their attempt at expanding their readership. But the project as it stands now exceeds my initial gesture of support; it is a tribute to the love of poetry, with a focus on film elements—since this is the medium Lynn and I work with—and it has certainly taken on a life of its own.

Kirby: We've been thinking about the installation as a way of eviscerating film, stepping into the film frame. There is no film itself in the space, only the elements of film—light and shadow, color, sound, the most basic lens in the form of a pinhole camera, acetate, the backing which holds the film emulsion, and of course, time unfolding.

The gallery contains a series of acetate screens, made of 5' wide by 16' tall panels, there are six panels across, in five rows of screens, the aspect ratio of 35-mm film—referencing a film projection screen, but also pages of a book. On the acetate screens are lines of poetry in reflective vinyl film. Motion controlled solarspot lights, mounted on vertical tracking/ pivoting motors—very non-digital—, are triggered by people walking through the room, and move much like natural light from the sun. Because the screens are of varying densities—clear, different amounts of neutral density and frosted—the light is transmitted through the screens differently and the words project from one screen to the next as well as on the walls of the gallery.

As the lights move, words, instead of images move in time through the space, casting patterns and shadows. The sound is not from a microphone that picks up what one would actually hear but from a *piezo* disk that picks up sound vibrations. For example, instead of hearing the sound of your own footstep you'd hear its rhythmic vibration, or sound pattern. Think of it as the interior of sounds, reflections of actual sounds. Those who make it to the end of the room can view a pinhole camera image showing pedestrians and traffic on the street in front of the gallery—the outside, the street, comes (upside down) into the gallery.

A: *I see, the individual making his or her way through the gallery eventually encounters the group. Are you trying to say that the personal and public intersect?*

T: Or the inside/outside, which is a way of experiencing the event. This is the very process of writing, of filmmaking, or of any creative exploration. Poetry, for example, is often erroneously thought of, in mainstream America, as an elitist language. Such a cliché still lurks in many righteous discourses, and yet as June Jordan has shown by founding Poetry for the People, or as Audre Lorde has repeatedly reminded, poetry as a practice is not a luxury. The act of coming intimately to language and to one's self is not the same as that of isolating or shutting one's self off, but that of opening up to the world outside.

K: We have tried to capture this in how we have worked with the materials. To make work, I have to go inside to understand my experience, to communicate that experience

June 10, 1999

T'ang Poem
for Trinh Minh-ha
after seeing and being
in
Nothing But Ways

word role wall fill Light
swell lock slide thrill sight
blue flow red turn tease
drape air wrap space bright

much love,
june jordan

I need to find where my own experience maps to the outside world. The lines of poetry on the screens reflect back when the light strikes, as well as projecting outward as shadows, they also refer both to an internal experience, to the body, and to film properties: "light, your intestines," "flick and flutter" and so on.

T: I should add that we're not trying to illustrate a poem or pay homage to any single body of poetry, but to create an encounter between film and poetry.

A: *Are you saying the film elements and poetry complement each other?*

T: No, because "complement" implies one element is submitted to the other. It's a relationship of subordination and domination—as in the way it's often said that a woman complements a man, or vice versa. Here, it's a question of creating another space where there's something of film and something of poetry, and yet this third space is neither one nor the other.

A: *While a film can affect a viewer sensorially, emotionally, and mentally, film viewing is essentially a physically passive experience. However, the installation you've created requires participation. Instead of sitting down and staring at a screen, the viewer must interact with the materials.*

K: We didn't want it to be the kind of spectacle that you sit in front of as you may with a film, although we want to make visible many of the properties of watching a film, ideas about framing, duration, the experience of changing light over time in space.

T: We didn't want it to be a spectacle, not only in the terms you mention, but on many other levels. For instance, rather than merely shifting the familiar context of a commodified object while still featuring the object to be looked at, in our installation, the space is part of the "artwork", and rows and rows of acetate—the screen/page—become passageways in which the viewer engages, tracing his or her own path accordingly, with the movements of light.

A: *This is the first time you have worked together on a project. What did each of you see in the other's work that made you want to collaborate?*

T: Lynn's work has always shown respect for the medium she's involved with. Most of the time people use film as an instrument; but in every film and installation Lynn made, the tools have been thought out creatively. I should add that while this is our first collaborative installation, we have collaborated before. We team-taught a core group of film students at San Francisco State. Lynn taught production and I taught aesthetics. Once a week, we met for a workshop, where the students would show their work and we'd all discussed it. Also, Lynn often came to see my work when I was in the final editing stage.

K: And Minh-ha would see my work. It's rare to find someone who can give you feedback at that point in a project when you are finishing and vunerable. I could rely on Minh-ha to be an open and critical viewer, I respect her opinion. She would help me to see the squirm spots—those areas of a project that aren't working. I've enjoyed her work for a long time as well. I admire how Minh-ha is willing to take risks from one piece to the next, to explore and experiment.

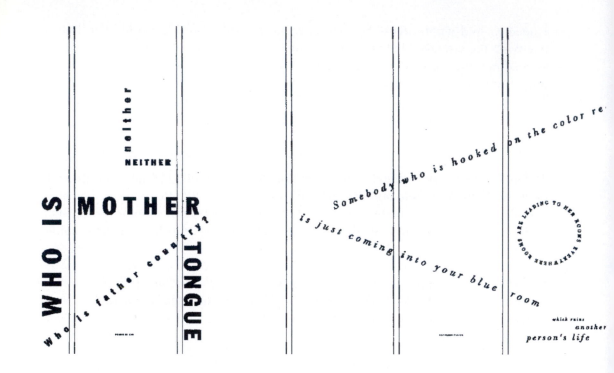

WHO IS NEITHER
neither
MOTHER
TONGUE

Who is father country?

Somebody who is hooked on the color re
is just coming into your blue room

EVERYWHERE ROOMS ARE LEADING TO HER ROOMS

which ruins
another
person's life

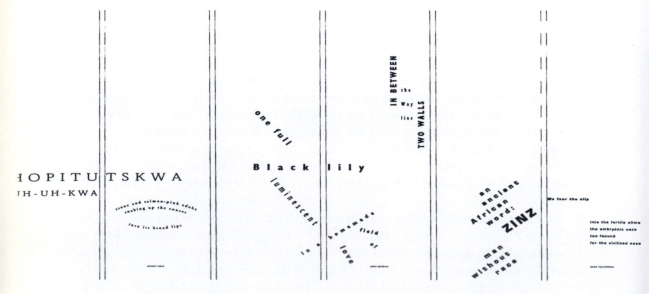

ḤOPITUTSKWA
JH-UH-KWA

stone and salmon-pink adobe
soaking up the sunset
into its broad lip

one full

Black lily
luminescent

in a homemade field of love

IN BETWEEN
the
way
lies
TWO WALLS

an
ancient
African
word:
ZINZ

man
without
race

We fear the slip

into the fertile slime
the embryonic ooze
too fecund
for the civilized nose

A: *What qualities or themes will those who are familiar with your other creative work recognize in the installation?*

K: My interest in light and space and time. Disjunctions, the space between the visual and the sound, through different forms or materials, I have been constructing indirect relations that connect sound and image to one another, yet leave them their separate spheres, this fluid space also leaves room for the viewer, and for the tale to unfold through time.

I enjoy working on the edges between "disciplines," between sculptural forms and film, between improvisation and installation, between live and recorded experience, between film and video, here between film and poetry—this of course, through the filter of understanding my life, and how to live in our changing world, the mapping of personal and cultural experience. I am fascinated with topology and systems and the screen as a window: the dance between the space of the tale, the surface or material itself and the act of framing.

T: My work, like myself, can be called "boundary events." They are events that happen at the boundary of different categories, cultures, and realms of expression. For instance, the categories of documentary, fiction, or experimental—what exactly is meant by "experimental"? Is it just a genre or is it a process in which we unknowingly engage, no matter what the perceived genre is, since it works on the notion of genre itself? And what is an installation? In *Nothing But Ways*, viewers are invited to walk into a dark space, to activate light, sound and words by their own movements through the piece and to participate in a concerto of reflections, projections, and vibrations. So what is it that we install ? Architecture? Sculpture? Music? Performance? And as the street also becomes part of the installation by way of the pinhole camera, is the gallery inside or outside? Attention is drawn to specific boundaries but also to their mobility. You'll find in my work the same importance given accordingly to image, music, silence and the verbal text. No one element dominates while the others are there just to illustrate. It's a heterogeneous space, whose social dimension is also to be found, for example, in the refusal to abide by a predatory concept of cinema founded on the supremacy of a central message or conflictual plot to which the whole film is submitted. Finally, there's the persistent questioning of the insider's and the outsider's position in terms of cultural politics. Each film, each book I come up with is yet another way to work at the difficult edge between these movements inside out and outside in.

SECESSION EXHIBITION: VIENNA, AUSTRIA, MARCH 8–APRIL 22, 2001

Installation: Adolph Krischanitz
Photo: Secession
Films exhibited:
A Tale of Love. 1995. 108 mins. Color
Shoot for the Contents. 1991. 102 mins. Color
Surname Viet Given Name Nam. 1989. 108 mins. Color;
B & W.
Naked Spaces - Living Is Round. 1985, 135 mins. Color
Reassemblage, 1982. 40 mins. Color

BETWEEN TWO

with Marina Grzinic

Edited from the public conversation with Marina Grzinic at the Secession, (Vienna, Austria) on March 7, 2001, for the opening of the exhibition/installation of Trinh T. Minh-ha's work—a project realized under Kathrin Rhomberg's supervision and Matthias Herrmann's presidentship. Grzinic's own experience and review of the exhibition, (first published in German as "Cinéma Boudoir: Trinh T. Minh-ha Film Installation—Secession, Vienna" in *Springerin* (Vienna, Austria), Vol VII, No 2, June-Sept 2001) is as follows: *"For the Central European viewer, spectator, and observer, the oriental, no matter how layered and powerful, is always connected to exoticism, surprise, and perplexity. Just as Eastern Europeans are seen as a brotherhood community of sex and killing, Asians and Africans are often seen through stereotypes of kinship, small paternal communities and situations of voicelessness. We, Eastern Europeans, no matter how near or far from the East, are perceived through a vast array of misinterpretations regarding blood, sex, and oppression. Why not force the viewer to enter the seraglio—not cinéma verité, but the cinéma boudoir.*

At the Secession, Trinh installed the five film works: Reassemblage *(1982),* Naked spaces—Living is Round *(1985),* Surname Viet Given Name Nam *(1989)* Shoot for the Contents *(1991) and* A Tale of Love *(1995). The viewer must remove their shoes before entering the seraglio. The idea was to have a simple but effective layout of several divided cinéma projection rooms in the exhibition space. Each room had a kind of sofa covered with pillows. Black curtains, heavy and plisse at the entrance of each projection space, functioned as veils. You want to watch? Come into the boudoir. Discover a world obfuscated by veils, much like our gaze. Trinh's cinéma boudoir questions our subtle formation as viewers in a way more powerful than cinéma verité, for each truth is covered by a veil. The seraglio is a hidden and dangerous place: saturated colors, elliptical narratives and out of context sounds. What struck me most was seeing all of Trinh T. Minh-ha's films at once—in a parallel mode. From one black box or veiled boudoir we are dragged to another, then, a third, a fourth. It is a vertiginous re-settlement of our thoughts, and not a pure, diachonically ordered excitement like the cinema retrospective. The synchronous time of viewing in this installation asks for film to be viewed in relation to film, in parallel tracks that produce a strange effect of de-realization. Each film is not simply the Other, but the Other of the Other; a kind of productive negativity, a frenzy of the coexistence of different time zones, histories, geographies, dramas, artificiality, dignity, postures, gestures—in one space at the same moment. In the public talk with Trinh after the opening at the Secession, I stated that the curator of the show, Kathrin Rhomberg, gave Vienna a precious gift by inviting Trinh to show her films. Could this have happened earlier? Was it too late? Never! A gift is always a pure sign of exchange, and a pure sign of a public politics. It is a point of reflection. If I try to summarize Trinh's manifold research in film, three key factors stand out. First, that her documentary films are keenly aware of their artificiality. They are sensitive to the interchange of fact and fiction. Second, is how making a film is in the end always a question of framing reality, progress, and interpretation. And finally, there is the metaphor of Vietnam and the consideration of the power struggles that take the place in the name of love, as in Trinh's film* A Tale of Love *(1995). The film was partly inspired by a Vietnamese poem written in the early 19th century, "The Tale of Kieu." In this tale a self-sacrificing woman must provide for her family through prostitution. Trinh's film transfers this story to the context of a Vietnamese immigrant in America. Her experiments with form are the basis of this film – e.g., lighting, scenography, camera movements, sound etc. through which she shows that such elements do not merely illustrate the meaning of the narrative. Lights, scenography, script . . . all have their own presence, logic and language. Each runs according to its own story. Much like in* Naked Spaces - Living is Round, *in* A Tale of Love *the color and rhythms of everyday life, are transposed into the film structure. In the end there is a rhythm somewhat similar to that found in the exhibition space, a multiplicity of sound and a labyrinth of curtains-veils.*

Grzinic: *I would like to thank Kathrin Rhomberg and Trinh T. Minh-ha for the invitation to this talk. When I was invited, I was thinking what a wonderful gift it is to the public to have the chance to see the exhibition of Trinh T. Minh-ha's work for the first time here in Vienna, at the Secession.*

Since I don't have a lot of experience participating in this kind of talk, I was thinking about how to start this event. If I would be in Ljubljana, I would say "I welcome you, Trinh T. Minh-ha, to Ljubljana" but I can't talk like this in Vienna because we are both strangers in this city. A very important point since this is what the work of Trinh T. Minh-ha is about: it is about being a stranger, about its positioning and about in-between relations and shiftings. Being a stranger is not a bad thing at all. We at least know that we are strangers. Others, in the context of Western capitalism, are faced with something much more horrible. At work here it's actually another kind of reversal, to find in yourself, in your most intimate position a stranger. So, in a way the subject is "colonized" already by the stranger within itself. Even more, it's this strangeness, this kind of emptiness and void that is the subject itself in the end. Another point of Trinh T. Minh-ha's works is that of strangers: the one that stays face-to-face with us, and the one within us, being estranged from ourselves. I think that parliamentary democracy raises a lot of questions concerning strangers and estrangements. These are worth taking into consideration especially since we are having a talk in Austria. The current Austrian political and social reality is captured by Joerg Haider, a controversial politician who praised elements of Nazi Germany. In the story of strangers we also have to take into account the situation in eastern Europe. I have a project called "East of East" where I deal with this story, and I deal with it continuously.

The work of Trinh T. Minh-ha is concerned with relations of that "between," that "shifting," that "nothing," and that "void." Today, this void is met by the drive to be filled by a kind of totality. Coming to this point, I would like to start our talk with a question about this in-between, this difference between stranger and estrangement, not only between these two entities, but as something that cuts within and opens the closed totality.

Trinh: To begin somewhere, perhaps I could link our being "strangers" to a reality that dominates our time: that of the migrant-self—a self whose condition is not merely defined by the practices of shifting habitats in relation to seasonal labor, and hence usually associated with foreigners; but a self whose dilemma is representative of postmodern times. Going from place to place, shifting borders, displacing identity are phenomena of our time; a time characterized among others, by mass refugeeism, immigration and homelessness. It's difficult to talk lightly about being a stranger and to romanticize that condition of the migrant-self. And yet, as Marina has commented here, the stranger is not simply the outsider or the foreigner from over there whom one confronts over here, in one's territory. Strangeness comes in many twos: between one culture and another, for example, but also inside a culture, between self and self. In other words, one needs to face what is strange in one. And one can say that if our situation— concerning race, class, gender, sexuality, ethnicity, religion, and other divisions—is politically so impossible today, it is precisely because we do not recognize the stranger within ourselves.

The stranger in oneself is what one tends to ignore and to gloss over. Hence the situation of democracy as Marina raised it, in which doors are claimed to be opened and differences seem to be explicitly recognized, while the people of the world continue to be squarely divided into two, Us and Them. One is constantly urged to align oneself. As it has repeatedly happened in political situations, one declares that, of course, one can tolerate the other and of course, one can work with difference. But as soon as one confronts the other in the flesh, one neither sees nor hears. For it is always possible to make do with the strangeness that is outside of oneself and hence easier to capture, fix and tame accordingly. But when this strangeness is intimate to oneself, it has neither name nor face that one can identify. So that the door of democracy, which is supposed to be open to multiplicity and differences, is actually a door only half open and carefully guarded. As soon as one faces one's own blindness and deafness, and sees the other intimately, one witnesses a different kind of strangeness—one that remains unseen, unrecognized, and unacknowledged to oneself. I would say that assuming the status of a stranger is assuming a site of unresolved difficulty, which can become a site of empowerment only when one faces one's other strangeness and remains a stranger to oneself.

G: *You were speaking about going from one space to the other and feeling a strangeness. It is very important to locate the space as a space in your work, a space to be re-covered in reality and in the space in which you live. It is interesting that in your latest book,* Cinema Interval, *this interval is related to time. Deleuze addressed this notion of the interval when he wrote on film history, and the classification of intervals in film history. In this work, space is placed in relation to time. Today, what matters when we use the computer and the Internet is a question of real-time. How fast we will be and in what time we will have access to what space? I would like to make a reversal and ask you solely about space. What is space in your films and what is the space of your theoretical work? How do these function in relation to the interval? How does the time of the interval refer to space, or simply, what is space for you?*

T: It's true that today's new technology demands as well as promises ever greater speed, the speed of light, as we now create in Megahertz. Always faster and more immediate. The gratification that one can get from such an immediacy is intense. Time and space are now conceived as inseparable from light. Rather than merely talking of cinema, and further, of D-cinema (digital cinema) as an experience of time, perhaps we can talk about it as an experience of spatio-temporal light relations. Spatial editing is how I see the montage work I carry out in creating that non-linear, layered, multi-spatial dimension in my films. The question of geophysical space is here reduced almost to zero; the urban and rural spaces of travel close in on the viewer's body. It's a phenomenon that has happened over time with technology. The image of the train speeding, which is one of modernity and of mobility, is an image often used to evoke a similarity with the filmstrip projected on the screen. From inside the train, however, the association that comes to me is that of the train rider as video viewer. A seated passenger looking out at these window images passing by; from this non-moving position, reality would strike me as one in which the division between outside and inside disappears. I'm then left wondering whether I am the one moving or whether everything I see is moving while I stay motionless in the same seat. Video and computer technology invites immobility all the while promoting mobility. Space is here experienced as temporal activity. Stay in one place and travel at high speed with light-images around the world.

In *Cinema Interval*, the interval is discussed both in cinematic and in musical terms. What's between two musical notes? As I've already elaborated, western musical education emphasizes the individuality of notes—their exact frequencies in production and reception—whereas musical practices in other parts of the world, in Asia and Africa for example, focus on the individuation of intervals. One doesn't tune an instrument to the standard A for example, one tunes it according to precise intervals. A note can be adjusted lower in one instance, and higher in another instance, but what needs exact tuning is the interval. As units of reference, intervals set the tone for the piece, while the notes' frequencies change as required by the circumstances. So it doesn't matter whether one sticks to the perfect A or not. One can go wherever one's voice or musical tool leads, as long as one maintains the interval. In other words, one listens to shifting relations rather than to fixed individual locations. And one can say that intervals are important because in performances, one is always playing in relation to. Often fundamental to this music is the human voice, which is a most precise musical instrument, and musicians would have to tune their instruments first and foremost to the singer's voice, while conversing with other instruments. It's all about relations and relationships—the time-space between two notes, two instruments; between musician and vocalist, or instrument and voice.

Although I did not discuss space per se, I did mention the related notion of spacing, which I also linked with rhythm, otherness and no-thingness, "Sounds are bubbles on the surface of water." John Cage used this image, for example, to designate the relation between sound and silence. We tend to focus on the event, the sound, the bubble, and what goes unnoticed is the always-there, the silence, the non-event, this vast surface of water from which bubbles come and go. Spacing is what allows one to face alterity in its omni-presence and absence. So to return to what I asked earlier, what's between two notes? What exists in a film, for example, between two images? What happens in the interval? The question mark is huge here, for every one of us would come up with a different response. It's a space of infinite possibilities. In other words, the interval is where we can ultimately say: "I don't know."

G: *Talking about space and intervals, how does this concrete museum space produce an interval within your works? In what way does the space of the museum correspond to the works and the way you arrange your films within it?*

T: Starting from "I don't know," I'll give you a glimpse into some fragments. (And this non-knowing, which is radical to the in-betweens of names, is not a question of relativism.) First, according to what happened yesterday with the opening of this event, with the way viewers moved from one film to another across the different fabric-enclosed spaces, I can reconfirm that I really don't know what is being established here in terms of relations in film reception. As a filmmaker, I have always made a clear distinction between film and video. To my financial disadvantage, I've insisted that my distributors not rent or exhibit any of my films in video format, because they are made as film and not as videos. Of course people can always go to video for analysis purpose or for personal viewing. But the first exposure to the work should ideally be an exposure to film, since each medium has its unique properties, and the experience of film is radically different.

This experience may escape many people, but for those of us working intimately with the materiality of the medium itself (rather than subordinate it to a story, a message or a spectacle), it's always a devastating experience to see one's work on video in public screenings. Not so much because of image resolution or of screen type and size— although these clearly do make a difference in the spectator's reception. We know that with technology the question of resolution can be solved. What is at stake is the difference that begins at the core, with the formation of the image itself. The film image is something well defined, that one can touch: a still, a frame, a rectangle, a piece of celluloid. Whereas with video, there is no real stasis, no "still" in other words; the image is in perpetual formation, thanks to a scanning mechanism. Such a distinction can radically impact the way we conceive images, which is bound to differ from one medium to another. Rather than experimenting with sequences of stills, one is here working, on both macro and micro levels, with the pulses of an ever-appearing and disappearing continuum of luminous images.

Now in this main hall of the Secession—an art space clearly not meant for film exhibition and in which filmmakers are still strangers and trespassers—I am given the opportunity to alter the space so as to have all five films shown simultaneously. Thereby, viewers can choose not only the order in which they see these films, but also the pacing with which to see them. Such a break with the preconceived linearity of more conventional film retrospectives has its advantages and disadvantages. People can stay as long as they want; they have a whole day for each film, and more if they wish, since the exhibition goes on for two months. Or, people can drift in and out, as dictated by the conventional walk-through gallery and museum art contexts. In other words, I cannot control the spatial and temporal condition in which they look at these films. One of the viewers told me yesterday that she had gone from one space to another, and that for the first time she saw a strong link between all of the films—something I could, in no way, foresee, even though with the body of work that one creates over time, there is inevitably a relation that emerges on its own from one work to another. Whether one is fully conscious of these links or not, they are created on their own, the way each film takes on a life of its own as it finds its audiences.

On the one hand, there is this element of the unknown that comes with the simultaneous screenings of the five films in an art space. On the other hand, there is also an element of the unknown that comes with a situation of collaborative and collective work. In order to minimize technical problems and to make possible the continuous projections of the films, I was asked to have them transferred to the DVD format, which is neither film nor quite video as we know it. In terms of image resolution, the transfer of all the 16mm films to DVD turns out quite well, the only one that really suffers is the transfer of the 35mm film, *A Tale of Love*. This being said, the difference between digital and analog video is here very relevant. For, what digital technology does provide is a bridge between film and video; it offers the possibility of going either way: of adapting the film look, or of keeping the video look, if not of shuttling between the two. Separating film's "unique properties" versus those of video no longer seems as pertinent, especially when one operates in this third terrain that is neither film nor video, as with the DVD, a format made primarily for projection.

Architect Adolph Krischanitz came up with this tent structure, which he designed to accommodate five cinema black boxes for the projection of the films. Here, the fabric serves both as curtains and as partition walls and ceilings. The floor is also covered in black, and the spectators stepping into the space (with their shoes off), walk blindly into one of the boxes ("sheltered as though . . . in the dark lining of a suit" as Krischanitz put it). Here again, we are dealing with an event that comes with a question mark: Is it architecture? Is it installation? Is it craft or is it construction? Is it a tent? Is it a movie hall or a series of theater stages? One goes from one box to another, opening and closing the curtains, and as one settles into the intimacy of these dark spaces, one slowly distinguishes, under the light reflected from the images, a bench at the center of the room on which one can sit or lie down. Departing from the set of the regular movie theater, such a structure or an envelope can act quite differently on the spectator's responses to the films. As you have suggested earlier, another kind of exchange might also be going on: since one can get so cozy and intimate inside these dark spaces and some viewers may linger on, late into closing time—because of the warmth, the pleasure and the open relations elicited by the encounter between the lying body, the pensive voices and the stream of luminous images—one may also wonder whether this is some kind of a bordello . . . Another possibility, which Kathrin Rhomberg has mentioned to me, is the link between this exhibition space and the market space outside. Every morning, to get from my hotel to the Secession, it is with joy that I walk through the market, amidst its rows of multi-color stalls and stands. So when I come in here what I also find at first sight are these mysterious stalls, whose stark exterior seems to enhance with even more intensity what is offered inside: to each space, a different world and a distinctive culture with its singular set of sounds and images.

Speaking of sound, if my work is spatial, it is also in terms of resonance. I'm not just talking about an aesthetic device that consists of increasing the sonority of a musical tone, for example—unless the ability to enrich and prolong a sound by supplementary vibration is here understood in the all-inclusive sense of the term. It is important in the creative process to acknowledge that one does not entirely control the movement within languages. As Walter Benjamin wrote, language communicates with language. In other words, it doesn't go linearly from speaker to listener, but once a word is released what it sets in motion takes on a course of its own, and the same may be said of images communicating with images. In my films, rather than having a subjectivity at the center that gathers meanings all around, you have a situation where the center is everywhere, and images, music and text unfold in an expanding field of relations whose self-generating 'rule' is that of resonance (and dissonance). How does a word resonate in different contexts? How can its repeated occurrence serve, for example, as a stimulus to undo contexts and make them shift layers with every coming and going of images?

There's always a little more and a little less than what is being said and shown. I do not know exactly how all these elements click in before the process of working with them. Hence, I do not function with a subject that preexists the image. Everything comes together only in the making process and one has to work very spatially in order not to lose the net constantly in progress—a weaving that is also a receptacle—and the captive resonance at work. In films dominated by linear time (the story line, the clearly aligned message), life's complexities are often reduced to a chronological line and to preconceived formulas of good and bad entertainment—the three-acts, made-to-order show with its clear beginning, development and ending. But with the work of resonance activated among the diverse elements of cinema, each viewer coming in and looking at the same film comes out with a very different response, depending on how they relate to the image, how the image speaks to them, and how images communicate among themselves.

G: *I think these different layers are a very important aspect of your work. When I look at your films I have the feeling that they are entities that think. Each film is structured in*

such a way that it's something that thinks by itself . . . it almost has something that I call a personal politics as an object. It has the strata, the functioning, and the different layers from writing, from music, from sound and so on, that it is almost thinking by itself within the structure. I'm always interested in these moments of generating meaning. In most of your interviews you point out very clearly that this is not a question only of technology. You use technology as a tool, but it really is a question of the meaning that is produced beyond the simple use of technology. So the way this body, this structure, these layers are actually filled and put together makes the film function as though it thinks by itself.

T: Two things are happening in this process. On the one hand there's the desire to share with the viewer, and hence the tendency to create something out of nothing. On the other hand—and this is much more challenging for me—the something one creates still retains its nothingness. The question is not so much that of giving form to something that has none before, which is what meaning strives for. If one goes after meaning, one is always trying to reach for a form. And the process of shaping in order to share is perhaps unavoidable since one needs a "something" to communicate with one's audiences. However, form is here only a step, for the nothing is all pervasive, like the surface of calm water whose incidental bubbles are the only things one sees. Whatever shape one comes up with is still nothing. Thus, form is addressed, but not for form 's sake; and the form reached is not a point of arrival. Rather, one reaches a form in order to address the formless, by which precisely, the form can manifest itself in all its vibrancy. This is why in my work there is no centralizing subjectivity.

People often compare my films to Chris Marker's. His is very fine work, and the rich meaning he produces in his films is marvelous. But his position is clearly that of a decoder. One can say that his projects are primarily based on a search for meaning, and his subjectivity, albeit discreet, is centralizing. Here lies the fundamental difference between our work, because in my case, not only decoding is not central to film as activity of production, but also, there's an emptying out of any center that tends to dominate, so that there's no core per se, only relations. Meaning is in constant flux. Elements of film and of the world move from their own centers; everything that attains form points to its own nothingness. This is where reflexivity in its emptying action also comes in, since you mentioned relations and conditions of production. Here, the creative process is always made tangible and visible, and the work, whose means and subject are presented as structurally mediated by the conditions and relations of production (that are also of representation), looks at itself in the act of coming into being. Such exposure and looking back opens into an abyss for one is constantly putting one's work at risk, as it can always return to nothing. So what does one see right there? A film, but a film about what?—That's the question people always ask, when they want to understand. We'll leave the question here to keep it alive, and we'll let it rise again with each work.

G: *You mentioned a crucial point—that the means of production have to be reflected as conditions of production. In most of cases, filmmakers do not expose this but leave it as something in the background. But the conditions and relations of production are crucial to why and how you make the film. In your case this point is always emphasized. It is part of the film, and is as well emphasized in your theoretical work. I think this is crucial: this* *is also how we can perhaps locate the difference with regards to what you were talking about in Chris Marker's work. This relation between the film, the means of production and the conditions of production is of crucial importance in your work.*

T: Aesthetics and politics go together here. The tendency to separate and divide is always looming large. What seems intolerable to the world of consumerism is the product whose workings retain an awareness of the conditions of its own birth. In mainstream criticism, whatever one criticizes is always conveniently located outside of oneself; one points one's finger at the other without that finger turning back on oneself. Such criticism is very safe, as it gives itself the license to judge without putting the judging and the judge at stake. Whereas to do critical work that takes away from you the ground on which you are standing is to acknowledge that when doors are opened, nobody is safe in criticism. Everyone is being taken in and everyone is involved in the challenge of that work—which my films solicit.

G: *This relation is part of your theoretical work as well. What is fascinating and very important, and in most of the cases makes people feel strange about your work, is that people do not know if you are a filmmaker or a theorist. You use your film works and your writings as part of discussions too. The structure that is behind your work is part of your theoretical writings. So it is not just a question of making a film, but it's a question of theory as well, or of theoretical writings. Both are doubling each other without taking the power out from each other. They are film and theory, simultaneously shifted. We think, 'Aha, the film, it's the meaning' and then we come to a theory and see it is actually a reversal of some film conclusions, and leads us to other questions. I think in this way the production of meaning is also deeply connected to theoretical discourse.*

Therefore, I wanted to ask about something you said once when you were giving a lecture: "It's very important in which situation you say: 'I'm a woman, I'm a feminist, I'm working on this and that." It's not just a question of preference, but it is always an absolutely political decision to declare in some public space in a very specific situation a very specific position: 'I'm a feminist.' According to this kind of position, when I was asked if I was a feminist I replied: 'No, I will not say that I'm a feminist from eastern Europe, but I will try to think about eastern Europe, about the whole paradigm that actually does not exist anymore, as a woman."

So, I want to ask you right now: Trinh T. Minh-ha, what is your position, how do you declare yourself, at this moment and in this room?

T: Well, first I'm voice and speech, and lots of silent breathing. What we're touching on, I would say, is the politics of naming. And it's not merely naming the other, but naming oneself that has become extremely problematic today, since the very name one is given through discriminatory practices is being politically re-appropriated. I've discussed at length elsewhere the terms involved in certain labels such as that of "feminist," or of "woman of color." Some people coming from the Third World would say, for example: "how foolish can they be, why do they call themselves people of color, why do they revert back to such a naming?" The same thing happens with "Third World," a notion that the very people concerned immediately reject, and yet it has been reclaimed as a highly politicized territory. When we use these labels on ourselves, when we call ourselves Asian American, or "Zami" (to borrow from Audre

Lorde) rather than Gay and Lesbian or Queer, for example, we are reclaiming a certain territory politically. So in that sense one would have to decide when to use what, and moreover, in the politics of new identities, questions raised are no longer confined to what and who am I, but they have expanded to include when, where, how, if, and . . . and . . . and . . ., in indefinite possibilities of combinations.

Certainly what matters is not so much whether I'm a feminist as how I am a feminist. With this in mind, it would be foolish to categorize oneself in a fixed way. In the same vein, it would be foolish for me to call myself "a feminist" when I am working with women in a village in Africa, for example. In this context, such identification only gives a false sense of political belonging as it keeps you apart from other women. But, if I'm in a situation where they are throwing stones at feminists, then certainly, I am a feminist. The politics of shifting identities is one that remains open to contingency and yet allows one to act. The fact that the oppressed or the multiply marginalized subject is always elsewhere than where she is able to speak from should not be confused with the fear, the refusal or the inability to take up a position. This is the fine line that we have to draw, because otherwise naming or not naming can be both apolitical and regressive. It all depends on how one engages the practices of naming in the struggle of positionalities.

In my writings on this question, I have used the term 'inappropriate/d other,' written with a slash and a 'd' which means both that one is inappropriate and one cannot be appropriated. The term still applies well to my relation with the Secession context as we've discussed earlier, and more generally, to my relation with the art world. In the brochure produced for this exhibition, I have also used the notion of "boundary event," which is not unrelated to the fact that rather than positioning myself here and now as a "speaker," I suggest earlier that I'm "voice and speech." My work and I are both boundary events. Boundaries signal at the same time endings and beginnings; there where one stops to exit is also there where one stops to enter anew. At best, the marking of a boundary invites a different kind of presence-ing, the beginning of a new space and a new fiction of identity. At least two movements happen simultaneously right at the boundary, and what comes out also comes in, what goes deeply in travels far out. This is how I see boundary events—events situated right at that edge of the many twos, where thinking is acting of and on both sides.

I have also at times taken on the position of the Blue Frog—a term borrowed from Elaine K. Chang, who when she was young was told a story about this frog by her Korean mother. The story was so compelling that even when she grew up and studied at the university she still remembered it. (I can hardly summarize it here without losing it.) One day, she asked her mother to tell her the story of the blue frog again—that was years after the mother had emigrated from Korea, and her English was a little bit better. The mother was quite confused at first, but after the daughter had recapitulated the basic plot to refresh her memory, the mother blushed and informed her daughter that there was, in fact, no blue frog. She had not mastered colors in English yet when she first told her the story. As blue and green bear the same name in a number of Asian languages, the mistranslated blue that makes all the difference in the story takes on a multilayered dimension. Old as she was, Chang said, she was crushed by the information that it was all along just an ordinary green frog.

G: *I would like to ask you about a possible counter process produced by the status of not having a name or of taking the name of the Other. It's coming very close to some research that I was doing recently on the Other—a topic you deal with in many of your theoretical texts and works. I was very interested in new possibilities of reading the Other and the One, developed through French theory, more precisely by Alain Badiou. When we put the Other against the One, it is obvious that the One needs the Other, but only because it needs to establish a demarcation in the field, otherwise there is not really a productive relation between them. This is why in such a relation the Other is just a negative of the One, its mirror image, so to speak. But we can give an another interpretation (I think it is important to give an another interpretation!) and think about the Other as not being perceived simply as the other of the One, but as Two. Two at the same time.*

That means we do not have the dialectics of affirmation and negation, but two parallel dialectics which are not coming one from the other, but are both present at the same time! Thinking about the Other as two, means to think about the world as something that has a double source, therefore it is not necessary to go back to the mythical one, trying to restore and build one history, one kind of theory, one big edifice. This means that actually other worlds on this planet and other paradigms can be treated equally. In such a constellation the History of the world is not the History of the lost mythical One, but a History with a double source, where several histories are coexisting in parallel, opening in such a way new possibilities for action.

T: Let me ask you, according to this theory, where you begin counting with two, the source is always two . . .

G: *Absolutely and I think this is very important. You start with the two; the two is the initial point and not the zero.*

T: If you start with two and there is no one, there is no zero either, right?

G: *That means, if I put this very shortly, that with counting (and this is where Alain Badiou is absolutely right) the One we will never take us to two. Counting as a method to come to the Other, is a male way, or the way Western Europe functions. It counts, one, two, three, states (Slovenia, Slovakia, Czech Republic, etc.,) will be part of the New Europe. The counted states are just the object of Western Europe's phantasy. This is why instead of saying it is the Other, Lacan says it is two (and here is where Lacan and Badiou are coming very near).*

T: I understand well this side of the question. When one looks at oneself in the mirror and one only sees one's reflection, then actually what one is negating is the function of the mirror itself. Because one does not allow the mirror to be mirror when one occupies that space. Starting with two allows one to break away from both that one-to-one relation and the notion of two as duality. Two is often thought of in terms of a dual polarity, in which the one is always against the other. In the past, critical theories have come up with such naming as the "Third space," "Third cinema", or as in my case, I've been referring to the "Third term." Here you are introducing this notion of the source itself being two. This may help to shift one's perception and the way one thinks about source, about origins, or about oneself—the same-self economy. And I've having speaking of many twos in our conversation. But there's also another side to the question: if one only starts with two, then what happens between two?

Even if one crosses out the one, what happens to the zero? In other words, what happens to the mirror right here? A great writer from Brazil, Clarice Lispector, wrote that only the one who is most delicate knows how to come into the space of a mirror without leaving her image on it. In other words, to look at oneself reflected, seeing the mirror at work rather than seeing oneself is to return to ground zero—there where the mirror is alive because it is freed of our traces. Mutual reflectivity ad infinitum. We have, on the one hand, this multiplicity—the place of differences—and on the other, this construed "one" likely to dominate our thinking and action—the ego, or the place of delusory power. But in between the two, or the many and the one, I think there is this third term, which one can call zero: an interval of no-thing. The one needs the zero(s). Zero is a necessary position; there where all numbers are possible when there isn't any. Zero is also a space. There are many ways to look at it. I've mentioned the mirror and its function. Only when the mirror is empty, can it reflect everything that comes into its field.

G: *Or the third term can be the Other of the Other.*

T: This is also a possibility.

G: *Even more, to say that the Other is two means not to explain the difference between the One and the Other, but to point to the difference immanent in the Other. The third possibility is the Other of the Other, that means that the surplus of two is not the third, but this surplus is already inherent in the Other. The Other of the Other means that the Other is not the double or the repetition of the One. So, the inclusion of the third possibility, is not a third possibility at all, but it is the auto-referential moment already generated through language. It is an inherent auto-referential moment in the Other, that makes it a non-whole.*

T: Which applies very nicely to the example of the mirror, since what the latter reflects are only reflections.

G: *Going back to the film The Tale of Love, it is interesting because a lot of criticism of this film claims that the structure and the way the actors relate to one another is too artificial. On the contrary, everything, not just the actors, are acting in the film; the sound, the color, etc. It's interesting that this criticism of the film's artificiality is based on some kind of natural relationship. But I found it much more interesting to say that sometimes an artificial relationship, if you think also about a love affair between two artificially produced entities, can teach us much more about love than any natural relationship. I'm very interested in the artificiality that you produce in the film, and its relation to the natural in terms of the border between naturalness and artificiality, if there is one. What and how much we can learn from artificiality about our natural position?*

T: It would be helpful to make a distinction between the different kinds of artificiality. One common way of looking at artificiality is to oppose it to the natural. The plastic, the synthetic, the foreign, the inauthentic, the imitated, the fake, the unreal; in brief, culture versus nature. A more inclusive way is to recognize that the natural still lies within culture, since both what we call natural and what we call artificial are "man-made." Historically produced, the real is a highly political construct. In this sense, artificiality cannot be opposed to naturalness, because it determines our everyday existence. And because we are living it all the time, it tends to go unseen. Humanized, mechanized, and computerized infrastructures have been transforming our economy, culture, and politics. We are, in a way, blind to the pervasive workings of "artificial" systems of control. To bring these to visibility, to put a frame or a boundary around them is not an "artificial" process, as commonly understood. It's simply to bring to the fore something that is already there but that one doesn't see.

For example, to show a film not as a product packaged for consumption, but as an event-in-the making that calls attention to its own processes, looks at the elements involved in its formation and exposes its performances as performances, is to see things simply as they are. As you nicely put it, "acting" is therefore not confined to the realm of actors, and every element of film—camera movement, framing, lighting, setting, color, music, silence, words and images—is an actor in itself. With today's new technology and with the phenomenon of virtual reality, artificial intelligence is an intimate component of our thought and work processes. Not only something produced mechanically and electronically can convey a level of emotion much higher than an imitation of nature can, as you just point out, but also, as media producers, we are already operating as simians and cyborgs, whether we acknowledge it or not. Cyberspace is a kind of black hole. No one can really avoid being sucked in. Ironically, in its immateriality, it's a place that has, for many of us, a very direct impact on our material situation. In other words, there's nothing more "artificial" in exposing acting as acting than in abiding by acting as imitating—or passing for real life. And if all constructs are seen as "artificial" then, many are those for whom the earth is primarily a human construct, for the ego is the largest construct we have come up with, one whose beliefs and delusions of power regulate our lives and the world of politics down to its tiniest details.

Moreover, there is artificiality in imitation itself. Such imitation, which does not recognize its own true nature, usually bears the name of "realism," and what people consider to be more realistic—not to mention more "real"—is actually a blind or deceptive artificial process. By imitating emotion, one sometimes kills the emotion, or else abuses it. Hence, resorting to the artificial as artificial with no judgement involved can help us recognize, for example, in our wiring systems our own nerve mappings. We can return to zero and be both one and two and more. I think emotion is very much a realm to be explored anew, because we have gone through a historical period where matters of the mind are set hierarchically well above matters of the heart, and there are a whole range of pejorative terms for everything considered to be sentimental. Exploitations of our emotions in love stories packaged for the market are common, so we have had to question such commodifying drive in the very instance of film consumption. In turning afresh toward emotion, especially in the realm of simulation, interaction and immersion, or of today's cybersensation, it is necessary then not to fall into the trap of psychological realism (which is commonly equated with depth). What is far more challenging for me is the work of exteriority—one intensely and passionately effected on faces, interfaces and surfaces (which are commonly equated with artificiality). Everything is seen "truthfully" and singularly from the outside, in recognition of one's limits, both through the mechanical or electronic camera eye (as differentiated from the human eye), and through the "artifices" of image-making. Acknowledged as such, artificiality often exposes what many of us take for granted as reality to be only one dimension of reality.

"Stone Alphabet," photo and body art by Jean-Paul Bourdier in *The Desert is Watching*.

THE DESERT IS WATCHING

Installation

Trinh T. Minh-ha and Jean-Paul Bourdier

Kyoto Biennale 2003
Kyoto Art Center, Japan, October 3–November 30

Photos projected, bodyart, and land art: Jean-Paul Bourdier ("Which side?" color insert following p. 170; "Stone Alphabet and "Heat," p. 212, p. 218). Video projected: Trinh T. Minh-ha. Photos of installation: Kunihiko Katsumata, Kyoto Art Center p. 219; color insert following p. 170), and Jean-Paul Bourdier (pp. 214; 217)

Twenty slides of painted bodyscapes in the Utah desert, one eleven-minute digital video of the Utah desert, two DVD projectors and one DVD deck, two slide projectors, stretchable cotton fabric, steel cables and anchors, one mannequin, one blue light, one green light.

In the desert, everything moves. Nothing is ever the same. To watch the light travel across the cliff, or to witness a lake shifting its location minute by minute with the wind's movement across the infinite surface of the salt, one has to dig oneself into a place and become a desert. Otherwise, in the desert, nothing moves. Sky power dominates. One walks into the silence of death and sees waves of mountains, rocks and sand with no movement.

The "desert" means different things in different cultures. In Japan where there is no real desert, it is said to retain its erotic and romantic connotation. The Gobi desert is said to evoke fantasy about exotic adventure, a fantasy that once functioned aesthetically as an inspiration to promote the Japanese invasion of China (Hiroshi Yoshioka). Widely used as a metaphor for urban inhumanness, the desert has been

largely revived today in the Western media as the very place where the enemy vanishes. As enemy land.

Every step taken in the desert is a step taken under watch. One goes there in search of "peace" and finds oneself tuning in with the mutability of the earth. The other who is our enemy is no other than oneself. Here the mind forgets but the body remembers: reptilian bodies, vegetal and mineral bodies standing still, walking, crawling, winding, rolling, slithering on rocks or sinking in the vast expanse of white. There, where there is no place to hide, one is found. The desert? It is what takes birth within, and paints itself on the watcher's skin.

This installation is the first manifestation of a larger on-going project whose realization will take on different forms in different locations and circumstances. As it is set up here, the spectators will not see any photo or video image as they enter the space. The fabric structure serves as a gradient device to slow down visual access. It is only when the viewers reach the second half of the room (or sooner if they are taller) and when their heads touch the fabric that they encounter, see, and experience images of the desert. Their intervention—either emerging above the horizon of the fabric structure or staying partially caught in it— determines the way they see.

The unstable, mutating video image-sequences, composed of long uninterrupted slow pans all moving in the same direction, offer a panorama of the desert in its seasonal appearances. The sequences are projected in pairs simultaneously on both sides of the wall.

The stable slide images are also projected in pairs as doubles, in shot- inverse shot, next to one another on the wall farthest from the entrance. They are shown in slow dissolves as mirage images that play with the relation between bodyscape and landscape.

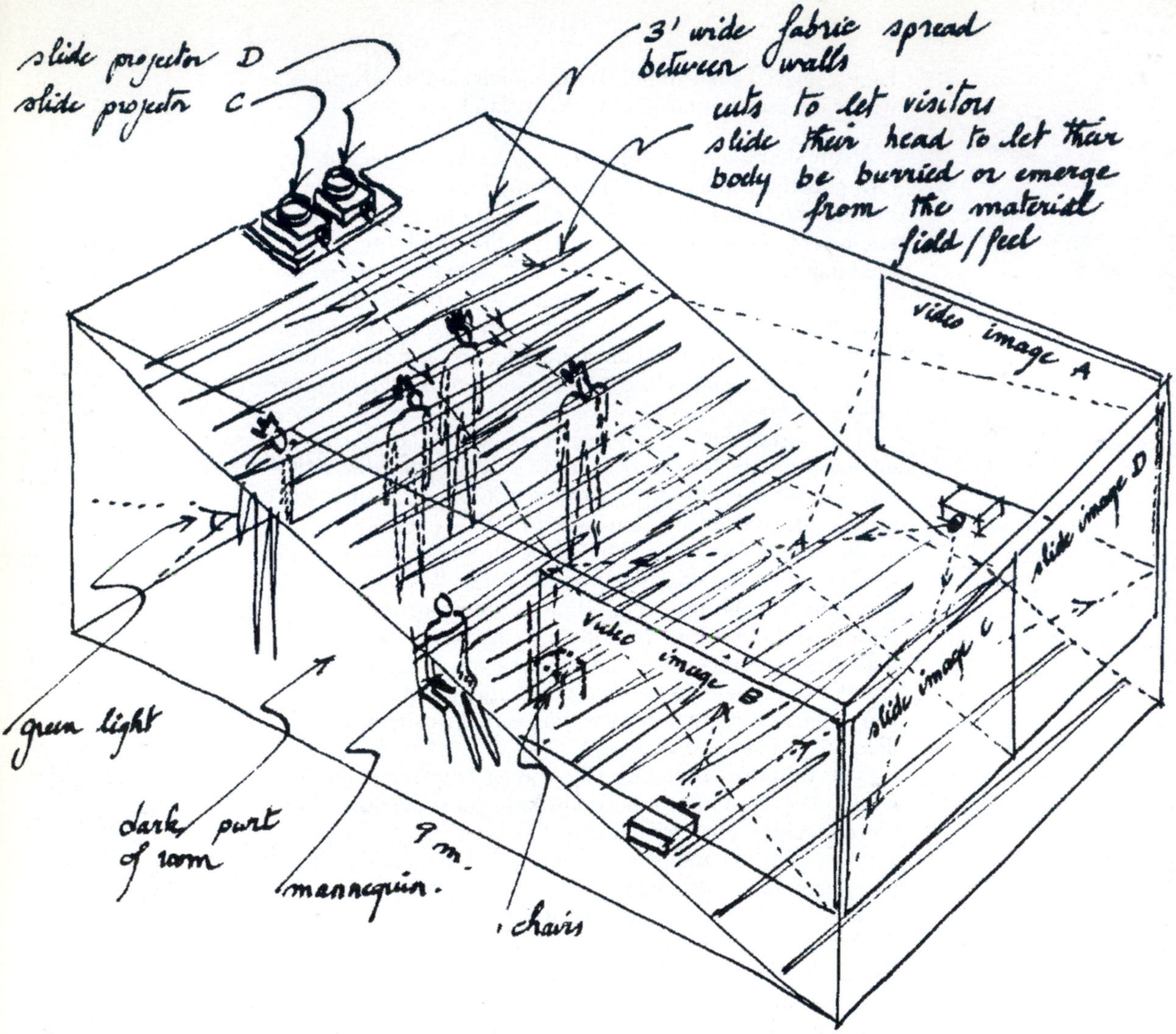

slide projector D
slide projector C

3' wide fabric spread
between walls
cuts to let visitors
slide their head to let their
body be burried or emerge
from the material
field / feel

video image A

video image D

slide image D

slide image C

video image B

green light

dark part
of room

9 m.

mannequin.

chairs

fabric through
which visitors
slide their head

mannequin

dark part of room

green light.

blue
light.

installation seen from the entrance

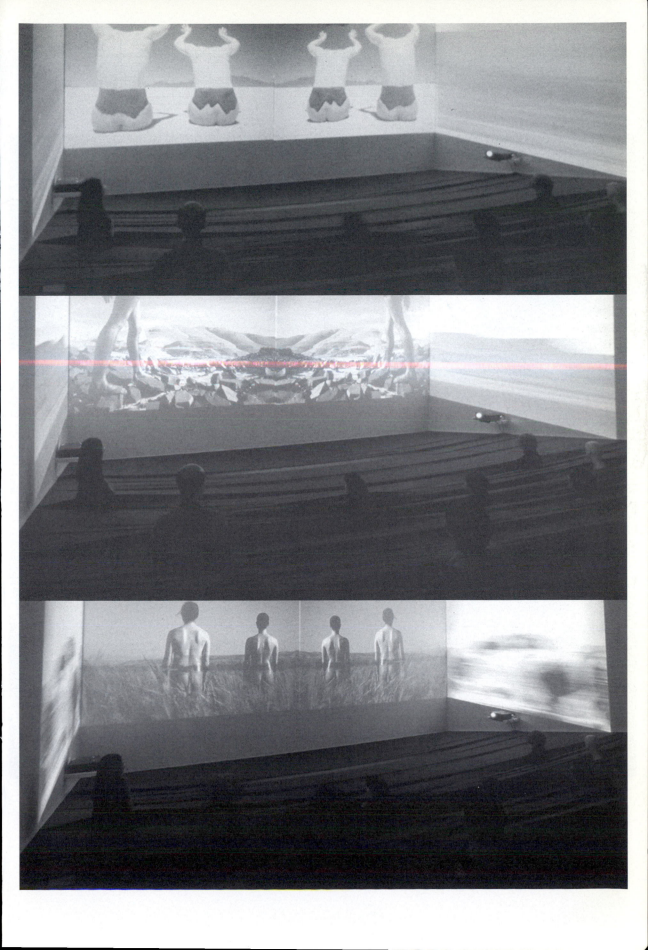

"Heat," photo and body art by Jean-Paul Bourdier in *The Desert is Watching*.

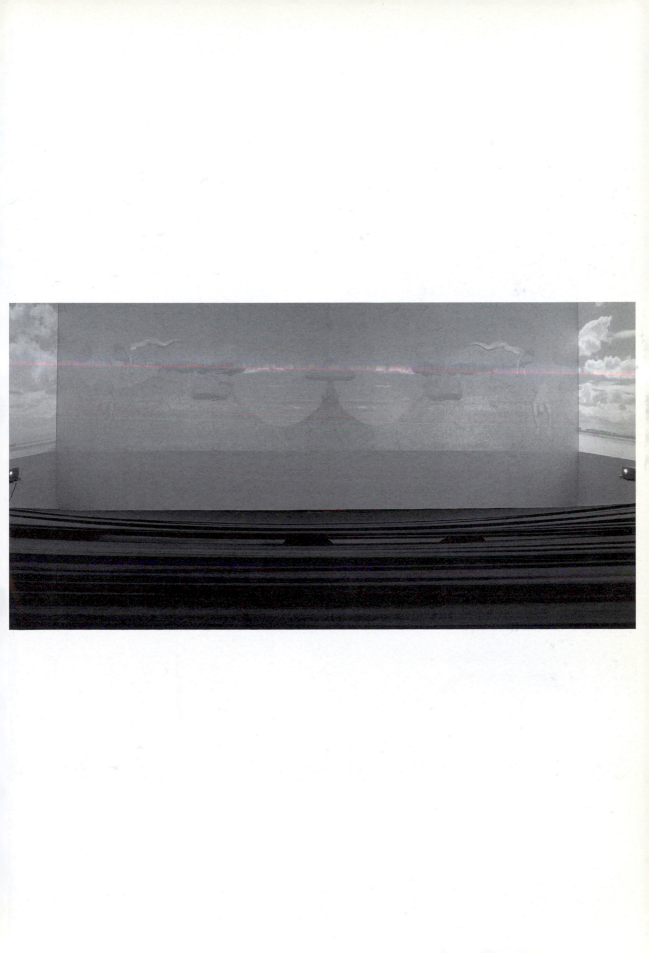